Reformation Riches
for the Contemporary Church

Reformation Riches for the Contemporary Church

Liberation for Both Skeptics and Burned-Out Evangelicals

DAVID BRUINS

WIPF & STOCK · Eugene, Oregon

REFORMATION RICHES FOR THE CONTEMPORARY CHURCH
Liberation for Both Skeptics and Burned-Out Evangelicals

Copyright © 2016 David Bruins. All rights reserved. Except for brief quotations in critical publications or reviews, no part of this book may be reproduced in any manner without prior written permission from the publisher. Write: Permissions, Wipf and Stock Publishers, 199 W. 8th Ave., Suite 3, Eugene, OR 97401.

Wipf & Stock
An Imprint of Wipf and Stock Publishers
199 W. 8th Ave., Suite 3
Eugene, OR 97401

www.wipfandstock.com

PAPERBACK ISBN 13: 978-1-4982-8149-2
HARDCOVER ISBN 13: 978-1-4982-8151-5

Manufactured in the U.S.A.   04/28/2016

Unless otherwise indicated, all Scripture quotations are from The Holy Bible, English Standard Version (ESV), copyright © 2001 by Crossway Bibles, a publishing ministry of Good News Publishers. Used by permission. All rights reserved.

Scripture quotations marked NIV are taken from the Holy Bible, New International Version, NIV. Copyright © 1973, 1978, 1984, 2011 by Biblica, Inc. Used by permission of Zondervan. All rights reserved worldwide. www.zondervan.com. The "NIV" and "New International Version" are trademarks registered in the United States Patent and Trademark Office by Biblica, Inc.

For
Maureen
Rebecca, Lauren, Emily and Joshua
& their families

and

for you

...and you will know the truth, and the truth will set you free.

JOHN 8:32

Contents

Note to the Reader and Acknowledgments | ix

Introduction: Christianity Is Really, Really Good | 1
    The Cultural Context: Beatlemania and the Contemporary Church
    A Quick Look Back in Time: How the Current Landscape
    of Protestant Churches Came About
    Current Realities

Part 1—Rediscovering Some Foundational Biblical Truths That the Reformation Had Also Once Recovered

  1 Why We Go to Church:
     Whatever Happened to the Divine Service? | 25
  2 The Law-Gospel Distinction | 31
  3 Easy as 1-2-3 vs. Just Shoot Me Now | 34
  4 The Gospel Is Objective and Powerful | 40
  5 The Gospel: More than We Could Ever Hope for or Imagine | 44

Part 2—How We Do Church: The Contemporary Protestant Evangelical Church Service and the Need for Reform

  6 For Members Only . . . Not | 51
  7 Restoring the Elements of Worship | 54
  8 Keeping Time with Two Calendars | 62
  9 The Bar Stool | 64
  10 The Mystical, Gnostic, Sentimental Christian
     (the One Standing out in the Meadow with Raised Arms) | 66
  11 Forgiveness Is Good for the Soul | 69

12 The Church Was Not Born Yesterday | 72

13 Music: The Great Exchange and the Need to Preserve Open Space | 75

14 Newsflash: The Bible Is Not about You | 82

15 The Message or the Massage | 85

16 More than a Message: Feasting on the Bread of Life | 89

17 Transcendent and Immanent Equilibrium:
The Geeky, Ultra-serious, Strange, Stoic, Lofty Syndrome | 93

18 Let the Little Children Come to Me, for to Such Belongs
the Kingdom of Heaven: A Pitch for Infant Baptism | 99

19 Creation, Vocation and the Two Kingdoms: Why Christians Can, and
Should, Spend the Week as Chefs, Stockbrokers and Special Ops | 103

Part 3—Some Additional Liberating Applications and Implications

20 The Railroad, AT&T and the Mega Church | 111

21 Neither Lone Ranger nor Cultish Commune: The Abuse of Small
Groups and the Communion of Saints | 114

22 The Way Forward: Ice Cubes or Icebergs? | 119

23 Getting from Happy Meals to the Healthy Plate:
Hypocrisy and Other Hurdles | 126

24 His Utmost for My Highest | 131

25 A Radical Me or a Radical Grace? | 134

26 Knowing and Doing God's Will in My Life | 139

27 The Practical Relational Implications
(Less Arguing, Less Frustration) | 142

28 Our Heavenly Inheritance | 145

Conclusion: Lennon and McCartney, John Paul, or John and Paul? | 156

Bibliography | 159

Note to the Reader and Acknowledgments

SO WHAT'S UP WITH a non-clergy guy from New Jersey writing a book about theology and Protestant evangelical churches? First of all, it's an interest that has been a part of me for a long time. Like Rachael Ray grew up around great cooking and Seinfeld grew up around great humor, thanks to my dad, I grew up around great theology. I guess it eventually rubbed off to some degree and just became part of who I am. Second, for better or worse, from Martin Luther and John Calvin (for better) to Charles Finney (for worse), those of us trained as lawyers seem to have a propensity for this sort of analysis. Finally, it's timing. Perhaps at no time in church history has there been such rapid, radical change in worship practice and focus as there has been in the past few decades. Add that to the massive changes of the prior one hundred and fifty years and we have a real mess. The great London preacher Martin Lloyd Jones, already in the 1960s, diagnosed that the problem with the state of the church was that it had been primarily preaching morality for the previous hundred years, instead of the gospel. Lest there be any misunderstanding, morality is not a bad thing. As we will see, it's simply that humanity's problems go so much deeper, and second, telling people to be moral does not and will not ever yield true morality.

Be assured that I don't presume for one moment to be a professional theologian. There are many who are much more qualified than I to deal with the subject at hand, and, who do so in a variety of ways. This book is simply a layperson's introduction to some topics which are very important for the health and well-being of today's church. I try to spell it out in everyday language from one layperson to another. To delve deeper, reformationriches.com offers a list of websites which not only provide a wealth of wisdom on these issues, but which also recommends various books, articles and online

Note to the Reader and Acknowledgments

resources. Most importantly, many of them can be an avenue to help locate a good local church for those in need of one. I'm just a beggar letting other beggars know where free seats are being offered for the banquet.

Partly due to my being fed a spiritual fast-food diet by the larger Christian community and also not being nearly as into the superb theology that had surrounded me while growing up as I should have been, I was sort of floating along until reality eventually caught up with me. I then found myself somewhat confused for a time about a variety of things happening in the church world and, consequently, in my world. Once it was all subsequently untangled for me, the whole world changed. I began to understand firsthand why the Protestant Reformation had rocked the world of the sixteenth century.

Having finally comprehended what it is to enjoy God rather than him being a threat or my judge, and understanding what it is to grow in the grace and knowledge of Christ, I can't help but share what I've learned. I hope to do so for the rest of my life. As the title of an old BeeGees' song put it: "I've Gotta Get a Message to You." *Yes, it's that good. Even if you've heard ten versions of Christianity that have failed you, I ask you to please read on one more time.* There really is a right version, a true and wonderful version, a version which is neither another performance-based hamster wheel nor another exercise in navel gazing, but which is utterly amazing—what Reformation theologians call "the Word rightly divided." Even though it was right in front of me my whole life to some degree, and though I had captured it to some degree, I wish I really "got" this stuff at a much younger age. The truth really does set you free. Besides, as an added bonus, even with everything that gets thrown at you in life, I would have been much more content on some important issues that were needless sources of frustration and stress for me. As a recovering burned-out Protestant evangelical myself, I'm continuing to learn more each and every day. So my prayer is that you, too, might understand more, sooner rather than later. Whether you are just curious or have been disillusioned by past experiences with a church, come rediscover Christianity at its best, from a historic, orthodox, classic evangelical, catholic (universal), Protestant Reformation perspective.

Besides my mother and father, I have to give special thanks to Michael Horton for so ably untangling the bird's nest of theological fishing line that had eventually come to entangle me and for surprisingly equipping me to do a little of the same. To Dr. Horton and the rest of the crew of the *White Horse Inn*: Kim Riddlebarger, Rod Rosenbladt, and former cohost Ken

Note to the Reader and Acknowledgments

Jones—thank you for teaching me so well as to why I should believe what I already believed, i.e., the very same things my parents taught me many years ago. Thanks, too, to Eric Landry at *Modern Reformation*.

To Todd Wilken and *Issues*, Etc., and your theological contributors, including but not limited to Bryan Wolfmueller, Chris Rosebrough, Jeremy Rhode, and Craig Parton, who daily serve up many of the rich ingredients of Christianity which have been missing from evangelicalism for some time. To Jonathan Fisk and *Worldview Everlasting* for keeping us up to date and connecting with the next generation. To David Zahl and *Mockingbird* for relating to the artistic and literary world. To the crew at *1517 Legacy* for your great resources. To Reformed Anglican Philip Veitch for fighting the good fight of the faith. With the caveat that I am not endorsing everything in any given book or on any website, including those I make reference to, thanks to all the innumerable authors and website bloggers out there for keeping the truth posted in love for all the world to see.

Similarly, to Tullian Tchividjian and the former *Liberate* contributors, thank you for bringing it all down to earth and making it so practical for every nuance of life. While I was doing the final edits of this book, Pastor Tullian had to resign his post at Coral Ridge Presbyterian Church due to a moral failure. I had quoted him a few times and was asked how I would now handle that. I have kept all of his quotes intact. His disqualification from the office of the ministry, whether temporary or permanent, does not change the truth or the beauty of his quotes. It only shows once again how frail we are as human vessels. Though yet imperfect, he's still a living miracle of God's grace. Thanks be to God through Jesus Christ our Lord who will ultimately rescue us from this body of death (Rom 7:24–25).

While they represent a spectrum of beliefs concerning the issues raised in this book, many thanks to the following for a lifetime of pastoral care and influence, both official (in churches where I was a member) and unofficial (in churches I had occasion to attend): Nicholas Monsma, John Van Ryn, Bernard Van Someren, Edwin H. Palmer, Joe Vugteveen, W. Robert Godfrey, Donald Wisse, Ray Van Der Laan, Richard Kuiken, Fred Provencher, Norman Brouwer, Peter Wang, and Deric Taylor.

Finally, thanks to Maureen, the love of my life, whose challenging me every step of the way produced a far better book than I could have ever written without her.

Introduction
Christianity Is Really, Really Good

THE CULTURAL CONTEXT: BEATLEMANIA AND THE CONTEMPORARY CHURCH

IT WAS A PERFECTLY beautiful, balmy blue-sky summer afternoon that began in a refreshing swimming pool. After a grilled dinner, it was off to New York City—over the George Washington Bridge and on to Yankee Stadium. I first had seen Paul McCartney in concert on a similarly beautiful day nine years earlier when he was turning sixty. Given his age already back then, I, as a late boomer (a.k.a. a Joneser), hadn't wanted to miss that opportunity to catch this twentieth-century legend in concert. When he burst into the Beatles' classic "Hello, Goodbye," I couldn't believe that I was really there witnessing a piece of history. When he sang "All My Loving," I couldn't have previously imagined hearing a live performance of a song he did with the Beatles on the Ed Sullivan show on black-and-white television when I was a little kid.

Now here we were nine years later as McCartney was approaching seventy and amazingly launching yet another tour, entitled "On the Run." The festive crowd that was gathering for this must-see concert spanned every generation. The excitement came to a crescendo as he came out on stage looking very much like a Beatle. He wore an early Shea Stadium–era Beatles-style suit jacket, in a later "Sgt. Pepper's"–era bolder color blue. His voice still rang out with that pure, clear, youthful trademark sound that had garnished all of those wonderful melodies over the years. His youthful energy was unmatched as he belted out about thirty-five songs for almost three hours without a break in a truly monumental performance. From my distant vantage point directly opposite him in the very middle at the very top of the grandstand, it just as well could have been McCartney back in the day. The stadium crowd was savoring the experience, grasping onto these last remnants of live Beatlemania before moments like these would slip away forever. Even McCartney intentionally paused and looked around for a moment to take it all in.

Life indeed can be very good. Christianity, at its best, appreciates all that has been created, unlike most other religions that have a disdain for the material world. As I took it all in, I found myself, as a Christian, asking a question: how exactly should the message Christianity be inserted into all this, besides giving us the ability to discerningly enjoy all of the graces of life common to humanity, such as good quality fun music? It's much easier to acknowledge the need for salvation when there's extreme nastiness or extreme poverty—both for others and ourselves. But what about for the nice and the self-sufficient? At times like this, when things are seemingly so good on the surface, it might just be a downer to suggest that we all need a Savior: nice day, nice weather, nice multi-generational crowd, nice concert. The last thing we need, it would seem, is for Christians to rain on this parade. Even John Calvin has remarked that man, in his fallen state as the progeny of Adam and Eve, has retained much, i.e., "is still adorned and invested with admirable gifts from [the] Creator."[1] But the progeny of Adam and Eve we are. As a result of their sin and our own against the God of the universe, things are never really, truly perfect in this present age, nice as they may be at times. Most importantly, we all live every day under a reality that lay just beneath the surface, the curse of sin and death.

McCartney outlived many of his contemporaries, including his wife Linda, Beatles John Lennon and George Harrison, and had managed to shine on in splendor for more years than most. With doses of makeup, to be sure, he had kept wrinkles, ailments and even death at bay. But the grim reaper of decay and death was not far behind. The crowd was in varying stages of aging and the big screen amplification of a 2011 McCartney showed that the effects of aging were starting to creep up on him as well. Only a year later, as he closed both the Queen's Jubilee in Britain and the 2012 opening ceremony of the London Olympics, it would start to become apparent that he was now becoming an old man. As with all of us, like

---

1. Calvin, *Institutes*, Book II, Chapter II, Section 15. (This particular section is well worth reading in full.)

Introduction

the name of his tour, he was truly "On the Run" against time. Though he would go on to release more great, even youthful, sounding music and perform even more incredible age-defying concerts for some years to come (thirty-eight songs / 3 hour concerts when approaching age 74 on his 2016 tour, e.g.), time does not stand still for any of us. It is this reality that we intuitively just do not want to hear. We would rather suppress the realities of death and having to stand unholy before a holy God than face them, even though a Savior has been revealed to us. As fallen creatures, we have a more serious flaw than we realize—an inbuilt aversion to receiving the diagnosis and treatment we need. We would rather just suppress these issues in daily activities and just fade away when we eventually have to die.

Most of my generation, including myself (as if that's not obvious), were fascinated with the Beatles and the whole phenomena of the 1960s and '70s. So why bring them up in a book addressed more to generations X, Y, Z and future generations? The fact is that many of the issues of the contemporary evangelical church, which we will look at, derive directly from the influence of the hippie movement of these decades. The cultural influence of that era cast a huge and pervasive shadow over the boomer generation and was extremely influential in the formation of the present culture, including the church. This is not to say that the 1950s were any kind of utopia. It was precisely the '50s own brand of moralism and civic religion that largely created the climate for the backlash of the '60s. The end result is that both the culture and the church that the Y's and Z's have inherited from the boomers is saturated with a disdain for anything institutional, a boomer worldview, and a very high priority on entertainment. While there is a long history of "low church" versus "high church," this movement created an aversion to any and all things institutional in the church, be they doctrines, formality, liturgy, authority, etc. This movement removed all vestiges of anything formal in evangelical Christianity and gave it a distinct hippie flavor. The boomer worldview really wasn't anything new; it was simply a lot of old pagan ideas common to humanity regurgitated and dished out by new prophet-musicians in a new age of ramped-up pop/rock entertainment. Ever since the Beatles' iconic and frenetic 1964 appearance on the Ed Sullivan show, every kid with an electric guitar or drum set has wanted to emulate that experience. God's good gift of musical entertainment increasingly became an established American idol. For church kids, the church sanctuary now would often become the perfect auditorium or theatre. It would soon come complete with a sound system, stage lighting, a big screen and a captive audience to boot. It was where garage bands could now become worship bands. As an eighth grader with an electric guitar in a four piece band in 1971, I recall the rush of our own five minutes of fame in the school auditorium. Before we knew it, our teacher had us appear in front of her church.

Though any number of musical entertainers could be used to demonstrate the propagation of this '60s and '70s worldview, the Beatles, as the biggest showbiz act of the twentieth century, epitomized it. While the Lennon/McCartney songwriting collaboration was the driving force behind the music, Paul McCartney and Ringo Starr were the less philosophically serious of the group. Their worldview sort of rode the coattails of a once Reformation culture. Extolling the working-class values of England, they basically sang love songs and other songs about the good and common things of life. George Harrison, on the other hand, essentially introduced Hinduism and the New Age to America. Besides Harrison, John Lennon was extraordinarily influential philosophically in the broader culture, which also found its way into the church, along with the new style of entertainment.

The Bible can actually help us understand where Lennon was coming from. As God's revelation to us, it gives us not only the true answers, but also graciously provides an amazing rescue to our true predicament. In doing so, it strikes a blow at our collective ego. It reveals to us that our natural state is fallen, and that our own natural solutions just won't suffice. Romans 1 to 3:20, in particular, describes in detail our natural fallen human condition. There it is revealed that we retain remnants of the knowledge of God and of right and wrong, but that, in our state of guilt, we tragically suppress the real truth about ourselves and about God. Rather than face our guilt before a holy God, we end up worshipping ourselves and our ideas. Because of our condition, without God's intervention, it is actually idolatry, in one form or another, that all seekers seek.

Therefore, what Lennon expressed through his music were the religions that naturally arise in the human heart in its fallen condition: both do-it-yourself moralism and gnostic/mystical inner experience. His Beatles anthem "All You Need Is Love" is that vestige of universal law written in all of our hearts. Everyone implicitly knows that we ought to get together and love one another. We're made for law and this one summarizes them. Exhortations to love, of course, are great as far as they go; however, in our fallen condition, we suppress the truth that we don't—and can't—love

Introduction

each other as we ought. We don't like to face this truth, especially about ourselves. When Lennon sang this song at the first worldwide televised "love-in" event, he was living a life that would soon include: leaving his wife, Cindy, largely abandoning his child, Julian, and, litigating with his bandmates. Despite his many other endearing qualities, all of this is a sober reminder that none of us really walks the talk. Truth be told, we more know this to be true about ourselves than anyone else.

Like sin, death also isn't naturally one of our favorite subjects. We will do almost anything to avoid facing the reality of this dark, approaching, inescapable storm cloud. The reality, according to Scripture, is that we are given seventy or perhaps, eighty years (Ps 90:10), that it is appointed to us once to die, and then the judgment (Heb 9:27; Dan 12:1b–3). If there is anything we are prone to suppress besides sin and the curse of death, it is the guilt of our sin and even the possibility that we, as unholy creatures, will face the judgment of a holy God. This reality, however, has been revealed both in nature and in Scripture, which further testifies to the reality of both heaven and hell. Lennon, reflecting the natural human heart, suggested that we should try to envision a different world with his classic song "Imagine." Reformed theologian and, ironically, close childhood friend of Lennon, Peter Jones, describes "Imagine" as expressing "the deep gnostic experience of liberation from the opposites."[2] Lennon (like Harrison), also extolled psychedelic and mystical experience in several Beatles' songs such as "Strawberry Fields" and "Tomorrow Never Knows."

Consequently, Lennon's legacy continues to be very easy for everyone to relate to; but he always seemed to have an awkward, if not hostile, time dealing with Jesus. His gaze was inward as it naturally is with all of us. In suppressing the extent of our predicament, we naturally look within, seeking to save ourselves by trying to ascend the slippery slopes of mystical experience and redeeming deeds. The good news of the gospel, on the other hand, comes to us from outside ourselves. In accomplishing its amazing rescue from sin and death, it exposes the truths we suppress, especially as to just how utterly hopeless we really are. Redemption does not naturally well up from within ourselves. It is a gracious gift from without. After the first couple of chapters in the book of Romans, referred to above, declares everyone unrighteous, it reveals a righteousness from God which comes through faith in Jesus Christ to all who believe. "Blessed are those whose transgressions are forgiven, whose sins are covered. Blessed is the one whose sin the

---

2. Jones, *Other Worldview*, 121. See also footnote 9 herein.

Lord will never count against them" (Rom 4:7–8, quoting Ps 32:1–2 NIV). Or, as Hebrews 9:27–28 puts the good news: "Just as people are destined to die once, and after that to face judgment, so Christ was sacrificed once to take away the sins of many: and he will appear a second time, not to bear sin, but to bring salvation to those who are waiting for him" (NIV). Only this can satisfy our deepest natural longing which Redeemer Presbyterian Church pastor Timothy Keller has referred to as "Home."[3]

To be clear, to make critical observations about Lennon's life and teaching in light of Scripture's teaching is not to judge him. That is always God's purview and his alone. As far as we are concerned, God teaches us to love everyone, including those with bad ideas. God does that all the time. His love reaches past all of our bad ideas. We know from Scripture that the mystery of God's electing love can save even a thief on a cross at the last minute of the eleventh hour. As a matter of fact, despite his enormously popular tunes such as "Imagine" which capture the universal, ordinary ideas common to fallen human nature, it is truly ironic that in the grand scheme of things, i.e., in God's providence, Lennon's lasting airplay legacy may well be his and Yoko Ono's beautiful Christmas song. In spite of himself and his answers that fall short, Lennon, along with Ono, the Plastic Ono Band, and the Harlem Community Choir, in "Happy Xmas (War Is Over)," unwittingly draws our attention to Christ, the rescue to true peace and freedom, through this song being played year after year. In any event, we are to love one another, irrespective of each other's beliefs. Though fallen, as fellow creatures we all bear the image of God. Moreover, it ought to sober "a wretch like me"[4] that I don't know who all those will be with whom I might be spending eternity.

So, to get back to my original question which I was mulling over at the McCartney concert as to how Christianity fits in, it is this. With Christ, life is not only good on the surface, it is good down deep and it is everlasting. Christians are not there to rain on anyone's parade, but to share that there is another parade that is both better and forever. *Christ saves us from that ever-present terminal disease of death and guilt that, even on our very best days, still lurks just beneath the surface.* While our natural inclination is to avoid these issues, the good news of the gospel is the greatest news in all the earth. In his grace and mercy God has revealed himself and his redemptive plan in the Bible. This unfolding plan initially culminated in the sending of

---

3. Keller, *Prodigal God*, 91.
4. John Newton, "Amazing Grace," in *Psalter Hymnal*, no. 380.

his Son, Jesus Christ, to redeem creation itself, as well as a huge multitude of people more numerous than the grains of sand on the shore and stars in the heavens from every tribe, language, people and nation by the power of his Spirit (Gen 15:5; 18:18; 22:17; 26:4; 32:12; Heb 11:12; Rev 5:9; 7:9).

Jesus lived a perfect life where both Adam and the nation of Israel had failed, thus earning for his adopted brothers and sisters the right to eat from the tree of life. He suffered, paid the death penalty to satisfy divine justice and conquered death by his resurrection so that people would have the right to be called children of God. His resurrection was as historically real as was the Civil War. Over five hundred witnesses saw him resurrected. After his resurrection and following Pentecost, twelve previous cowards were inspired to willingly endure being beaten, jailed and most of them crucified themselves. Their passion was to go and address, head on, humanity's natural, self-destructive avoidance and denial issues and to share this must-hear news with the rest of the world. As this news still continues to be spread, he takes our treasonous spiritually dead selves, giving us mouth-to-mouth resuscitation by his Holy Spirit. He writes us into his last will and testament, making us coheirs with his Son. He will fully restore his children one day, in body and soul, for eternal life in a new heaven and a new earth, to be reunited with him, truly at home in his very presence. In cosmic terms, the decisive battle has been won, the stock market has skyrocketed and a family is being reunited. In short, the gospel is a lot of very good news.

In the age to come there will be no deluded suppression of the truth and no more having to keep running from the end, for there will be no end. We need not be devastated by the passing away of the good things he gives us now for our enjoyment. They are but glimpses of what is yet to come in the age to come. The Maker of the heavens and the earth is the same Maker of cultural talent, even popular culture talent—whether it's John Lennon's and Paul McCartney's voices and melodic genius, Michael Landon's acting and screenplay abilities, or the voices of Karen Carpenter, Amy Winehouse and others. He will one day restore all things to true and utter perfection, forever.

This is the central message and sure hope that the church again needs to herald to the nations. Unlike Lennon's answer for the nations in "Imagine," an old nineteenth-century Protestant hymn called "When Morning Gilds the Sky" puts the answer this way: "Ye nations of mankind, in *this* your concord find, may Jesus Christ be praised."[5] The gospel is the greatest

---

5. "When Morning Gilds the Sky," in *Psalter Hymnal*, no. 322 (emphasis added).

story ever told. These are the words that speak a new creation into being. Then, as hearts are stirred and quickened, people can take hold of the gift of eternal life. It is in the promised coming age that the best music ever will forever be played and heard, a place where no one grows old and where there will *never* have to be a final concert.

All of this was the glorious and unique message that the early historic Christian church conveyed through the preaching and sacramental delivery system which God had ordained. When the medieval church went off the rails, it was the Protestant Reformation that restored this message and means of delivery in the church. Sadly once again this great rescue message is no longer being heralded as it ought to be in many Protestant evangelical churches today. At best, the good news has been watered down and diluted with the religion of this passing age. In trying to contextualize and accommodate to the culture, the church, like previous times in church history, has actually appropriated much of the religion of the culture. The church, in seeking to appeal to the present culture with the music of the present culture, is often finding out that much more has, and is, happening to itself in the bargain. *Today the church's ecclesiology—how we do church—often looks a lot more like a Beatles'* Magical Mystery Tour *of experiential, mystical entertainment rather than the biblical model of being graciously addressed by the Triune God through preaching and sacraments. The church's theology— what the church believes about God—often looks a lot more like "All You Need Is Love" moralism rather than our being rescued for not loving as we ought to.* In clear contrast with the deficient wisdom of this passing age, the church should be conveying the greatest hope ever known to humanity. Instead, the church finds itself having taken on much of this "wisdom," often rendering itself indistinguishable at its core from the rest of the culture.

The boomers' entertainment-driven influence, their anti-institutional influence and their substantive philosophical influence in the church now inherited by the Y's and the Z's cannot be overstated. The decades of the '60s and '70s created a culture dominated by entertainment, fostered a hostility to the institutional church, and made paganism look really, really cool. This is the marinade in which much of contemporary pop evangelicalism has been saturated. These new assumptions are a substantial part of the legacy left by the boomer evangelical church to succeeding generations and have become part of the established order for much of evangelical Christianity.

Introduction

A QUICK LOOK BACK IN TIME: HOW THE CURRENT LANDSCAPE OF PROTESTANT CHURCHES CAME ABOUT

Before beginning a discussion about the Protestant church in contemporary America, it is necessary to understand at least the basic history of where we have been. Therefore, we begin by taking a brief look at the current lay of the land and how it came about. This should assist the reader who has had any exposure at all to Protestant Christianity. It will help identify where you might have been and where you might now land in the vast spectrum of Protestant churches. Even reading through a quick thumbnail sketch of the Protestant church's history of the past few centuries can be a little daunting and tedious. If you really dislike history, you may be tempted to skip this part and go directly to the next section; however; if you can stick with the history for just a few pages, it will greatly help in your understanding of the rest of the book and of today's churches in general.

There are three major expressions of Christianity in the world today: the Eastern Orthodox Churches, the Roman Catholic Church and the Protestant Churches. The first two groups resulted from a split in the church between the east and the west in the year 1054. The third group, the Protestant churches, originated as churches protesting against, and seeking reformation of, the medieval Roman Catholic Church during the early 1500s in what came to be known as the Protestant Reformation. Led by Martin Luther and then John Calvin, John Knox, Ulrich Zwingli and others, the reformers protested that the Roman church had lost its way and that a return to biblical truth in key areas was needed. The Protestant label is still used today to broadly refer to those churches that are not Eastern Orthodox or Roman Catholic.

Over time, a vast and confusing array of Protestant churches has developed. In order to understand today's maze of Protestant churches, one needs to go beyond their denominational labels and analyze them in light of the major contemporary paradigms that now exist. While the denominational labels reveal something of a church's history, they will likely be of very little value in describing it now. Churches today that may share the same historic denominational label such as Lutheran, Presbyterian or Reformed, are often extremely different from one another. Moreover, many contemporary churches have now shed their denominational labels altogether. Whatever their label may or may not be, the major contemporary paradigms for American Protestant churches can now basically be divided into three broad categories. Take any Protestant church today of any denomination, or of no denomination, and it will generally fall into one of these three categories.

The theologically *liberal* churches comprise one category. These are made up of the old mainline denominations which are now remnants of the once influential mainstream, mostly Reformational denominations that they once were and that were prevalent in the early American landscape (i.e., Episcopal, Methodist, Congregational, Anglican, Presbyterian, Lutheran and Reformed). Heavily influenced by both the Enlightenment and Romantic eras, these churches, over time, largely forsook their own written confessions and the good news of the gospel as it was historically understood. They usually deny one or more of the fundamentals of the faith such as: the divinity of Jesus, the inerrancy of the Word of God, sinful human nature, the substitutionary atonement, the miracles, even the bodily resurrection of Christ, his future bodily return, and that salvation is through Christ alone. Their identity became more concerned with liberal political causes, soup kitchens, afternoon concerts and art exhibits. Jesus' identity became merely that of example, friend and teacher, rather than Savior.

There is also a newer hip, reheated version of this same phenomenon. The *emergent* church is basically theological liberalism reincarnated in a postmodern form. The former group tends to be elderly and high culture. The latter tend to be younger and eclectic. Both tend to be, at least in part, reactions against forms of pietistic fundamentalism with their initial emphasis on inner feelings and subjective experience over creeds and confessions of faith. "Repeatedly in the past few centuries, we have seen how easily an inward-directed pietism and revivalism turns into the vinegar of liberalism."[6] Emergents exhort people to be "Christ followers" irrespective of what one believes. Invariably, when one's primary identity is Christ follower, rather than believer in Christ, Christ's identity morphs into that of merely a good example rather than our Savior. Liberalism is an aberration of classical, orthodox Christianity and cannot properly be called evangelical. It has essentially lost the evangel in the classic sense of the word. A unifying organization of this group of churches is the National Council of Churches, which, during its heyday and up until 2013, was headquartered in New York City.

While the need for reformation in Protestant liberal churches is very apparent, this volume does not primarily focus on this group of churches. Identifying them at the outset does help clarify the identity of the other two

---

6. Horton, "Your Own Personal Jesus," 18.

Introduction

groups to which this book is primarily addressed. Therefore, when we refer to *Protestant evangelical* churches, it is the following two groups of churches to which we are referring: *American pop evangelical* and *Reformational* churches. As a caveat—as with all categorizations, there are always plenty of exceptions. One can still find more theologically conservative evangelical churches among liberal denominations and one can find theologically conservative evangelicals in liberal churches. Often the liberal influence begins with the leadership and works its way down to the pews through a steady diet over time. Moreover, from a human perspective, it can often be a rather hazy prospect to identify when a liberalizing church actually crosses the line into liberalism and can no longer be called evangelical.

The second major category of today's Protestants can roughly be described as *American pop evangelical*, though it has its *Pentecostal, fundamentalist dispensational, neo-evangelical, contemporary church marketing* and *emerging* variations. Many of this movement's roots can be traced back to the more extreme views of the reformer Ulrich Zwingli, as well as the radical Anabaptist fringe groups already present at the time of the Reformation. While all of America's older denominations were originally Reformational with European roots, John Wesley, in the eighteenth century, broke rank and founded the Methodist church, institutionalizing three huge changes: free will Arminianism (a theology named after the views of Jacobus Arminius); allowing the ordination of pastors without formal seminary training; and teaching that one could obtain perfect sanctification in this life through a "second blessing." All of this was opposed to both the Lutheran and Calvinistic teachings of all the Reformational denominations for the preceding centuries. Wesley worked the small towns and rural areas and this uniquely spawned American (and English) religion spread like wildfire on the frontier with Methodist, and also Arminian Baptist, churches being established all across small-town America. While the Methodist Church itself has since digressed into mainline liberalism, these Wesleyan ideas still permeate American evangelicalism.

Then there were the even more extreme innovations of the revivalists of the Second Great Awakening in the 1800s which comprised the church's first marketing movement. Big-tent revivalists such as Charles Finney, Billy Sunday, and D. L. Moody would travel from town to town like the circus, combining entertainment with preaching. Theologically, the revivalist movement was characterized by legalistic moralism and mystical pietism (eventually, and ironically, fueling both future liberals as well as conservative fundamentalists).[7] The focus had shifted from God and his doing, to the people and their doing and their inner experience.

By the beginning of the twentieth century, there were more changes. A splinter group would identify Wesley's idea of a "second blessing" with "speaking in tongues" launching the *Pentecostal* version of this American religion. Also, a new end-times doctrine and way of interpreting the Bible, which emphasized discontinuity between the Old and New Testaments, had developed known as *premillennial dispensationalism*. Moreover, in reaction to the developing liberalism of mainline churches, a group in 1910 had published booklets called "The Fundamentals: A Testimony to the Truth," which defended some basic fundamental doctrines that were being eroded by the liberals. Having been influenced by the Romantic and Transcendentalist movements of the late nineteenth century, both the inward directed pietism of those secular movements, together with Anabaptist-rooted separatist ideas, helped to create a *fundamentalism* largely isolated from culture in the early twentieth century.

Post-World War II evangelicals such as Billy Graham, Carl F. H. Henry, and Harold Ockenga sought to change that by encouraging greater academic and cultural engagement by evangelicals. This became known as the *neo-evangelical* movement. This branch of American pop evangelicalism is the most similar to the category of the Reformational churches discussed below. *Christianity Today* magazine was founded as a cooperative forum for these groups.

In the 1970s a large politically conservative group comprised of individuals from all of these evangelical groups, led by pastors Jerry Falwell and Pat Robertson, became identified as the Christian Right in much the same way as liberals became identified with the Christian left. Additionally, beginning with California's Pastor Chuck Smith, the hippie generation began to influence evangelicalism with its own brand of "Jesus people."

By the late 1970s and 1980s new revivalists would seek to apply business models to church growth, launching the church growth or *church marketing* movement, also commonly known as the seeker-driven movement. Beginning with Robert Schuller, Bill Hybels and then Rick Warren, Christianity became a commodity to be marketed to the public and the megachurch was born. Drawing largely on the social ideas of business management guru Peter Drucker, these churches were deliberately designed to look and sound less churchy and more like entertainment venues.

---

7. See ibid., 18–19.

Introduction

Traditional elements of worship were replaced by more mystical music and sermons consisting of practical tips for living—all designed to meet the "felt needs" of the consumer. Denominational labels were dropped from the names of these churches and replaced with newer hip-sounding generic names. Embarrassed by the evangelical label, many simply call themselves Christian, ignoring the reality that there are categories of Christian churches defined by beliefs and practices. Publications like the *Leadership Journal*, the *Purpose Driven* curriculum, and Willow Creek Leadership conferences became very influential. The role of a pastor was often largely redefined to that of a CEO with pastoral work increasingly delegated to lay quasi-shepherds (middle-level managers) of organized small groups within the larger organization. While growth was promised, these churches largely prospered by emptying more traditional churches. According to most statistics, evangelicalism overall did not grow and may have actually declined.

By the 1990s the postmodern-era *emerging* children of the boomers were already reacting to the individualistic and splashy entertainment of these mega "Walmart" churches, creating their own variety of the megachurch. They sought to establish authentic and transparent communities more in the "Starbucks" style. "Emergents" would liberalize as described above, while the "emerging" would try to retain the evangelical faith, yet seeking to be particularly relevant to a postmodern culture. One branch of the emerging church is the Acts 29 network, a church-planting movement of "New Calvinists" that represents a fusion of some key Reformational theology discussed below with Wesleyan/evangelical/emerging methodology. Also, the Gospel Coalition website was created as a more contemporary joint forum for neo-evangelicals, Reformationals and emerging in much the same way as *Christianity Today* still functions. Contemporary outgrowths of the Pentecostal movement have included the errant word-faith televangelists over several decades and the more recent errant prosperity (health and wealth) gospel proponents like Joel Osteen, Creflo Dollar, T. D. Jakes, and Joyce Meyer.

As can be seen from this whirlwind historical recap, there are older forms of American pop evangelicalism represented by fundamentalist dispensationalism, Pentecostalism and neo-evangelicalism, and newer forms of American pop evangelicalism represented by the church marketing and emerging movements, as well as various mixtures of all of them. Many today are quite justifiably concerned that American pop evangelicalism's shift, particularly from fundamentalism and neo-evangelicalism, to church marketing and emerging megachurches has left it weaker and shallower than ever before and, therefore, very susceptible to sliding into liberalism in the near future. Even as this book is written, a convergence with theological liberalism is clearly underway in much of contemporary pop evangelicalism. A unifying organization of the American pop evangelical churches as a whole has historically been the National Association of Evangelicals.

Finally, the third category or paradigm of Protestants (and second category of Protestant evangelicals) would be that group of *Reformational* churches that didn't either liberalize or go pop with the waves of revivals, but sought to be true to their confessions and the good news of the gospel. These churches are evangelical in the classic sense of the word. They hold to the fundamentals, but are not merely fundamentalists. They have a very rich and comprehensive understanding of the faith. At the time of the Reformation, the various denominations had formulated written confessions setting forth what they believed Scripture taught concerning things central to the faith, in addition to the very basic creeds of the church, i.e., the Athenasian, Nicene and Apostles' Creeds. For example: the Lutherans developed the Book of Concord, containing, among other things, the Augsburg Confession and Luther's catechisms; the Anglicans had the more abbreviated Thirty-Nine Articles and the Book of Common Prayer; the European Continental Reformed, the Three Forms of Unity (Belgic Confession, Heidelberg Catechism and the Canons of Dordt); the British Reformed (Presbyterians), the Westminster Confession of Faith and its associated catechisms; and, the Baptists, the London and Philadelphia Confessions of Faith. What we are referring to as today's Reformational churches are often also described as *confessional* or *confessing evangelical* churches, because they continue to abide by their confessions as faithful summaries of the teachings of Scripture.

Generally these churches tend to be alternative denominations standing in contrast to their more liberal mainline counterparts. In the past they have been smaller in numbers, but continue to either grow or hold steady in contrast to the rapid decline in numbers being experienced by their liberal counterparts. Examples would include the Presbyterian Church in America (PCA) as distinguished from the mainline liberal Presbyterian Church in the United States (PCUSA). Likewise, the Lutheran Church Missouri Synod (LCMS) stands in contrast to its liberal counterpart, the Evangelical Lutheran Church in America (ELCA) (very confusing that they would call themselves evangelical!). There are numerous smaller Reformational

Introduction

denominations such as the Orthodox Presbyterian Church. Also, on the Reformed side, the United Reformed Church (URC) stands in contrast to the largely liberal and declining Reformed Church of America (RCA). The Christian Reformed Church (CRC) can currently best be described as a conglomeration of liberal-leaning, pop evangelical and some remaining Reformational influences, depending on the individual church. Many of the leaders of the Reformational churches over recent decades, which have, in fact, retained their evangelical identity, are also familiar to and have provided much leadership to the American pop evangelical community as well. These leaders have included: J. C. Ryle, J. I. Packer, John Stott, Donald Grey Barnhouse, Martin Lloyd Jones, Francis Schaeffer, C. Everett Koop, R. C. Sproul, James Montgomery Boice, James Warwick Montgomery, Leland and Philip Ryken, D. James Kennedy, Timothy Keller, Michael Horton, and Todd Wilken. Like American pop evangelicalism, this category of churches has also had its fringe elements, such as the misguided theonomy movement.

What is remarkable in looking at the vast majority of these churches, which have sought to retain their confessional or Reformational identity, is how much they hold in common in their confessions. Theologically conservative Anglicans, Baptists, Presbyterians, Reformed, and Lutherans together have carried forward many of the essential biblical truths recovered during the Reformation. Many of these churches, however, have been watered down over time and do not follow, in practice, what they officially hold to on paper. Looking at most Reformational churches in their diluted state today, it's hard to see why the sixteenth-century Protestant Reformation turned the world upside down. A good part of the reason for this, no doubt, is due to the pervasive influence of Wesley and Finney in American evangelicalism generally; however, much of the compromising of biblical truth is simply due to the default settings present in every human heart. In any event, many have embraced the newer forms of American pop evangelicalism, especially the church marketing model. Others have been mired down in legalism and traditionalism for the sake of traditionalism. As a result, while some of these churches already have the treasures discussed in this book, most need reforming to the same degree that pop evangelical churches do. Most, if not all, of the remedies discussed below, are actually already written in the historic confessions of these churches. There's just a lot of dust covering them right now.

Furthermore, using the words of Thornton Wilder, Paul Zahl observes that good words can sadly become "degraded or defaced" sometimes requiring "new persuasive words" for old gems of truth.[8] God's words never change, but ours do. Think how names for babies keep changing over the generations. Cutely named sinners like "Myrtle" grow up, give their name a bad rap and, eventually, it goes extinct until a new generation rediscovers its original meaning. In the recent past, for similar reasons, the words "Luther," "Calvinist," and "Reformed" have conjured up negative images for some; therefore, while these words often do present such a challenge, there are new generations now starting to take a fresh look. A unifying organization of Reformational churches is the Alliance of Confessing Evangelicals.

CURRENT REALITIES

There are particular times in redemptive history when succeeding generations do lose their way. In the Old Testament there was the generation that arose that "did not know the Lord or the work that he had done for Israel" (Judg 2:10). Similarly, the medieval church, over the course of many generations, descended into a dark period of confusion. I believe that, for large segments of the contemporary Protestant evangelical churches in America, this is one of those times. While the self-destructive state of the liberal churches has been obvious to many for several years and is not the focus of this book, it is astounding to fathom the seismic changes which I have personally observed over the course of just a few decades in the American pop evangelical church and also their influence on the Reformational churches, particularly as a result of the church marketing and emerging movements. Important and glorious truths obvious to Christians of my parents ("greatest") generation are virtually unknown to my children's ("millennial") generation. The church marketing movement of the boomers and gen X, led largely by Bill Hybels and Rick Warren have utterly changed the American church landscape. The so-called worship wars between the church marketers and traditionalists appears to be over. The new church marketing paradigm has swept through the American Protestant evangelical churches like a tidal wave.

I grew up in what then could still be called a Reformational denomination, the Christian Reformed Church. This was the same Dutch immigrant–orientated denomination that Bill Hybels grew up in (as did Harold

8. Zahl, *New Persuasive Words*.

Introduction

Camping, as well—now there's a stray missile that is another story!). I completely understand what Hybels and others were and are reacting against. While the doctrine was sound, it was often delivered in a joyless, stifling way. There was often an erroneous assumption that worshipping in awe and reverence, as the Bible teaches, meant that the minister could not smile or otherwise ever express joy or cheerfulness during the service. Second, there were often heavy doses of legalism in many of these churches. Moreover, there seemed to be a disconnect when it came to reaching out to our neighbors. Even where there was attempted outreach to "outsiders," attempts to facilitate their being taught and discipled were often rather awkward. For the first twenty-five years of my life, I sat in a worship service where the same people, except for gradual changes due to births and deaths, gathered every week and basically sat in the same pews. While that reflected an admirable generational fidelity in the passing on of the faith, it was undercut by a lack of or very weak local outreach. This introversion was no doubt due, in part, to the fact that all Reformational churches, by definition, were immigrant churches in a new country. But they took far too long to Americanize, much less to catholicize. There needed to be a more vibrant outreach in the pubs, cafes, and homes with genuine discussions stimulated by Christians commonly sharing the reason for the hope within them. This would have naturally resulted in some skeptics at least visiting church services as a more common occurrence. The fact that this did not occur created such a backlash that the church marketers have now embarked on turning the churches themselves into nightclub and cafe look-alikes.

Providentially, I had remarkable exposure to some of the Reformational and neo-evangelical giants of the past generation. My dad, who was in charge of "pulpit supply," i.e., arranging guest preachers for our church, invariably invited one of his mentors, Dr. Edmund Clowney, president of Westminster Seminary, Philadelphia—the same person referred to by Timothy Keller as his mentor.[9] Westminster was a pinnacle of Reformed

---

9. Timothy Keller dedicated his book *Prodigal God* to Edmund P. Clowney. In the introduction, Keller writes that "the foundation for my understanding of [this biblical text] was a sermon I first heard preached over thirty years ago by Dr. Edmund P. Clowney. Listening to that sermon changed the way I understood Christianity." In the acknowledgments he writes, "As I got to know him over the years he also taught me that it was possible to be theologically sound and completely orthodox and yet unfailingly gracious—a rare and precious combination" (xii, 134–35).

As I was completing this book, I discovered yet another amazing connection regarding Dr. Clowney. Following their close friendship and sharing a desk together for five years at the Quarry Bank High School in the 1950s, two lads from Liverpool, England,

Christian higher education. As a kid, I completely squandered what could have been a golden opportunity to listen up to some priceless wisdom and didn't pay all that much attention. By college I was paying a little more attention and my personal mentors included: the late Edwin H. Palmer, who coordinated the NIV translation of the Bible and had begun the work on the NIV Study Bible before his death; the late professor and former US congressman Paul B. Henry of Calvin College (who was the son of Carl F. H. Henry, first editor of *Christianity Today* magazine and often called a father of modern neo-evangelicalism); as well as Dr. W. Robert Godfrey, who would later become president of Westminster Seminary, California. Being personally exposed to these teachers gave me a profound appreciation for the Reformed faith that I don't think I would have had from simply being catechized (taught) in the normal routine of growing up in a Christian Reformed Church.

What really blew me away in more recent years, however, was the realization of how little I understood of Reformational Christianity, even with these influences. The American pop evangelical culture has had such a pervasive influence, it had unconsciously affected so much of my thinking. Moreover, when the church marketing movement began to flood virtually all of the churches, including the denomination I grew up in, I instinctively knew there were serious problems inherent in this movement beyond those which were obvious and which I couldn't always put my finger on. Feeling like the floor was being knocked out from under me, I knew I could no longer just whistle my way through. I began to search out good Reformational resources in order to understand exactly what was going on and to learn how to untangle the many twisted knots of this new phenomena. What I then learned was truly astounding. As the glorious and liberating truths of Reformational Christianity were finally made clear in all their alpine glory, I realized that I, and much of the Reformational church, were largely ignorant of many central biblical teachings which were actually recovered during the Reformation. So many of these great treasures had been lost not only in recent decades, but in the last few centuries, as well. The church

---

would part ways and proceed in two very different directions. John Lennon would go on to embrace many of the ideas of Eastern religion, while Peter Jones would go on to unpack the glorious truths of Reformational Christianity. After the University of Wales (BA), Gordon-Conwell Theological Seminary (MDiv), Harvard Divinity School (ThM), Princeton Theological Seminary (PhD), and marrying Dr. Clowney's daughter and Wellesley College student Rebecca Clowney, he would go on to become a leading Reformational theologian in his own right.

Introduction

marketing movement was just the second of a one-two punch in the contemporary era. The first punch was the first marketing movement known as Finneyism or revivalism, which left many churches seriously diluted over the past one hundred fifty years. Consequently, what many of us had been defending as "traditional" or "Reformed" or even "biblical" church was severely lacking and, in particular, was invariably highly legalistic. As deficient as the church marketing movement was and is, given this deficient version of the "traditional," "Reformed," or "Reformational," the worship wars would and could never rise above their own terms to produce a true reformation.

Therefore, much humility is needed in addressing the inadequacies on both sides of the debate. We are, after all, ultimately on the same team. While both the zealous intentions of the church marketers and the steadfastness of the traditionalists has been admirable, the fact of the matter is that we all leave a mixed legacy. As the Reformers taught, in this life we are simultaneously saint and sinner, not yet perfected. "The good news is not the mark we leave on the world, but the mark God leaves on us in baptism,"[10] i.e., uniting us to Christ, sealing us with the baptism of water and Spirit. He is the one reconciling the world to himself. This is the real drama of which we are privileged to be a part of as recipients and heralds. He is the one building the kingdom, not us.

To that end, this book is a collection of some of those vintage liberating treasures that were recovered during the Reformation and which have again become lost in our generations. Again, some were lost as a result of the influence of the old American pop evangelicalism of the late eighteenth through twentieth centuries; some were lost much more recently as a result of the newer forms of American pop evangelicalism of the past few decades. Just as the first Reformation rescued a generation from the darkness of an obscured medieval Christianity, it is my hope to make a small contribution to a new reformation by passing on some very important things that nearly passed me by. A new reformation is urgently needed to unveil the glorious and liberating truths of the gospel that have been all but totally obscured in current Protestant evangelicalism, both American pop and Reformational. Granted, there is no such thing as the perfect church, but the prevailing Protestant evangelical churches out there today should and need to be much more faithful in the basics. Instead of fostering inner-directed mysticism and works righteousness, they need to once

---

10. Horton, "Missional Church or New Monasticism?," 21.

again recover their role as heralds of the good news through which God has promised to dispense the glorious riches of his grace. As we will see, evangelicalism needs a fresh infusion of Reformational, sacramental and mission-minded churches—churches that neither fall into the trap of being stoic and legalistic, nor which are captive to the seeker-driven entertainment / small-group megachurch model.

Very often today people say they don't care about good doctrine because, despite our differences, we'll all be in heaven together someday anyway, so it really doesn't matter. The Scriptures, however, teach the opposite on the importance of doctrine (meaning teaching) and offer much more than deferred benefits (Matt 23; Heb 13:9; Eph 4:11–16; 2 Tim 4; John 21:17; Matt 7:15).

We are given the privilege now to enjoy God and grow in the grace and knowledge of Jesus. We don't have to wait to start growing. God wants us to thrive spiritually here and now, both in good times and in severe hardships and persecutions. To say that we will not be given a theological SAT on the way into heaven is absolutely true, but it completely misses the point when it comes to why good doctrine is important. God wants his sheep to be fed and well cared for now. He does not want his flock to be malnourished nor left wandering in dangerous areas vulnerable to the attacks of predators. For example, if you believe it's ultimately up to you to save or transform the world, whether it's physical poverty or spiritual poverty, your life will become a very slavish existence. You will end up functioning much more like a child of the slave rather than the child of the free woman that God graciously intends (Gal 4). Similarly, if you are trying to "connect" with God, whether it's through your service, your experience or your speculation, you will invariably find yourself connecting with an idol of your own making rather than the God revealed in Scripture. Likewise, if you try to view the world as consisting of only the holy and the profane, you will miss out on the whole third category of reality—all of the good, common, ordinary gifts God provides to believers and unbelievers alike for our mutual enjoyment and edification. Moreover, if you happen to be a minister, you are giving the sheep a significantly deficient and distorted message if you never smile while feeding them—even if you get all the facts right! We'll discuss more about these kinds of things later.

The point here is that he wants his gifts and graces for you to be clear and not obscured by clouds which we, by nature, perpetually create, irrespective of which church paradigm we find ourselves in. In the end, doctrine has very practical effects. Not all teaching that is labeled Christian is the same. Some accurately reflect the teachings of Scripture and some do not. Many of the teachings in pop evangelicalism today—as well as in the compromised state of Reformational evangelicalism—tend to leave people very confused, burned-out and often neurotic on many issues and in many areas. It often creates either self-righteous pharisaism or despair—or sometimes both. Even worse, people walk away from the church thinking that the lame version that they have been fed is what Christianity is all about. If the essence of Christianity is what is depicted in movies like *Saved, Salvation Boulevard,* and *Higher Ground,* I'd walk away, too. God desires better for his children. He has much greater gifts to give.

Whether it is described as recovering treasures of gold, removing the clouds to reveal the clearest and bluest of skies, replacing fast food with delectable and healthy cuisine, or coming out of the valley to behold the most amazing alpine splendor, rediscovering the glorious biblical truths that were recovered during the Reformation is extraordinarily liberating and invigorating. Whether you are a victim of endless cultic "small group" abuse, legalistic traditionalism, a casualty left in the wake of the latest mega pastor's "fastest growing church" or just plain tired, the thoughts that follow are not meant to be read and then forgotten among many other books which have become lost in obscurity on seminary library shelves. Hopefully these thoughts will serve as a conversation starter to help direct the church's attention to the many rich, readily available, Reformational resources that have been prepared by individuals far more qualified than me. These resources are the salve that needs to be to be soaked up like a sponge for the utter healing and reforming of the church in America as we know it. There is nothing more important in all the world that I could pass on to the next generation, including my own children and grandchildren. Christianity is good—really, really good. I wouldn't want anyone to miss out and have to settle for the deficient versions out there that, despite all the smiles and the hype, will more often than not, leave you cheated, frustrated, exhausted, and perpetually neurotic. Many of us are, by nature, neurotic enough already!

PART 1

Rediscovering Some Foundational Biblical Truths That the Reformation Had Also Once Recovered

1

Why We Go to Church
Whatever Happened to the Divine Service?

THE DIVINE SERVICE: I vaguely remember hearing these words a few times during my lifetime as the historical name for the worship service. Even when I more recently learned what these words were all about, I assumed this title had long been extinct. I hadn't realized that there was still at least one Reformational denomination that had preserved it in many of its churches to the present day. The first time I set foot in a Lutheran Church (Missouri Synod), I was utterly amazed to find the Lutheran Service Hymnal actually still called it the Divine Service. After participating in the service, tears of joy literally flowed from my eyes on the way home. Ever since that first time and the paradigm shift which resulted for me, I cannot wait for Sunday to roll around and so look forward to going to a good church. At no time in my life before can I honestly say that was the case. Yes, I would usually attend church on vacation when no one was looking, but it was much more out of a sense of duty than desire. There is probably no more important a chapter in this collection of short essays for the church today than this one.

This paradigm shift I experienced wasn't so much about the more liturgical style, although there is much that can be recovered in that regard as well; rather, the paradigm shift concerned the basic elements of what was happening, who was doing what, and, that the primary direction of the service was the exact opposite of what I had come to believe. It was in the Lutheran Divine Liturgy that I clearly recognized the elements of worship, specifically God's activity of showering the people with his gifts and graces.

Part 1: Rediscovering Some Foundational Biblical Truths

These elements had more vaguely existed in the Reformed services of my childhood as well as in other Anglican and Presbyterian services that I had occasion to attend. The vagueness I had experienced often resulted from an over emphasis on worshipping correctly (obediently) in accordance with Scripture at the expense of an under emphasis of why that was important. It often became all about doing it right for the sake of doing it right. It was eye opening to realize that God put in place his ordained means of worship as means of grace precisely so that he could draw near to sinners and give to us his gracious gifts.

In the past few decades, evangelical church services in general, including Reformational churches, have increasingly slipped into becoming human-centered rather than God-centered events. I guess there's no surprise here, since it is part of our very nature to make everything about us. As a result, these elements, that were formerly present, are largely absent in most contemporary worship services. Across the board, church services have largely become constant drones of exhortations for us to do more and try harder as opposed to recounting what Jesus has done for us. Churches vary in what to do more of, and, what to try harder at. For more conservative churches it may be private and public morality, for more liberal churches, social justice issues, and, for more charismatic churches, having an inner experience. Undergirding it all is a constant exhorting, all of which only ends up puffing people up and/or burning them out. It never provides the actual nurture needed if there is any hope of doing more and trying harder at anything.

A good first question to ask ourselves is: Are our church services primarily about Christ and him crucified or are they are primarily about the Christian, i.e., us? Who is being maximized as awesome—us or Jesus? Then, even when we can acknowledge it should properly be first and foremost about God, we usually still have a way of making it about us. Therefore, a good second question to ask is: Who is the main actor in the service—God or the people? That is, even if the focus is shifted away from our narcissistic selves and our problems to God, is it then still all about our addressing God as opposed to us being addressed by him?

Basically the evangelical church has somehow gotten it all backwards on both counts for some time now. Our problem is that we are going to church primarily for the wrong reasons—for us to do something for God, to experience God and/or to speculate about God. These reasons which we commonly have for worshipping are precisely the three ladders of idolatry identified by Martin Luther: the ladder of good works, the ladder of mysticism, and the ladder of speculative knowledge. Church becomes our means of attempting to ascend to his throne or of trying to reach up and to pull him down to us (Rom 10). Even good things then become distorted and turned into idols. Worship becomes all about our service to him, our "building" the kingdom, our being missional, our changing the world and making it a better place, our "connecting" with him through praise, our efforts to emotionally and mystically experience his presence, and our finding ways to speculate about him through inner contemplation. But who are we that we can give God anything? What do we have that we did not first receive?" (Rom 11:35; Job 35:7; 41:11, Ps 50:7–15; Acts 17:25; 1Cor 4:7).

The Reformation had recovered a biblical sense of worship opposite to that of "the work of the people," the medieval mass. In short, the assembling in God's presence was all about *receiving* his gifts. Through Word and Sacrament, God's saving power was poured out for the justification of the unconverted and the sanctification of the converted. The gospel was the power for salvation, both justification and sanctification. As Ruth and Billy Graham's grandson and former Coral Ridge Presbyterian Church pastor Tullian Tchividjian has observed, the gospel "not only ignites the Christian life, but fuels it [throughout] as well"[1] (Gal 3:3). *Much like a service station, the "service" was God's service to sinners*. It was first and foremost about God delivering the benefits of his work accomplished on behalf of the people. Worship then included echoing back praises, prayers and offerings to God following his demonstrating his worth-ship yet again. Michael Horton likens it to ministers breaking open the piñata and the people being showered with God's grace every week. *It was like sitting at a lavish Thanksgiving feast or unwrapping a plethora of amazing gifts under the Christmas tree.* This was also similar to the way many Psalms are patterned, which is what God's people used in worship throughout the Bible. It is after recounting God's great works of grace and mercy that there are the responsive praises of the people in the Psalms. God clearly is to take the lead in the dialogue of worship.

The gifts would be lavished upon God's people through Word and the sacraments of baptism and the Lord's Supper. Like Peter, we naturally resist him washing our feet, yet he reminds us that unless he washes our feet, we have no part in his kingdom. We, like Peter, can then respond, "Lord, not my feet only but also my hands and my head!" (John 13:8–9).

---

1. Tchividjian, *One Way Love*, 213.

Jesus then responds, reassuring him (and us) not to worry as he already has that covered. Through baptism and then in the absolution, or assurance of pardon, given weekly as a present-tense reminder, we are ever washed and re-clothed with the righteousness of Christ. Through the Lord's Supper we are fed, united to the vine, our very source of nourishment. Through the Word, we are further addressed by our Heavenly Father and thereby fed with the Bread of Life. *You actually can look forward to going to church like a good vacation, a day at the spa and a sumptuous meal at your favorite restaurant. Spiritually you come to receive a good bath, a nice hot meal and a fresh change of clothes. More profoundly, it's another effective treatment for the residual cancer of my sinful nature with, yet again, the joyful ongoing sure and certain promise of ultimate and complete recovery.*

So how did the church lose its direction? Probably the same way it usually does. The kids complained that church was boring. Parents responded with the sentiment expressed in John Kennedy's famous saying "Ask not what your country can do for you, but what you can do for your country." In this context, however, it was to ask not what God can do for you, it was you who needed to do something for God. So it was taught that we go to church not to "get" something, but to give, i.e., to serve. Now there is a sense in which the expectation of "getting" can be wrong. Jesus desires disciples, not consumers. In relation to God we are all beggars, not shoppers. The church is not like a shopping mall where Jesus is there to meet our felt needs. He is there in the hospital for sinners to give us what we really need. He is there in the law office reading the will, describing and distributing the vast riches of our inheritance as adopted children. We need to learn from him as good disciples and receive that which he has to give, not what we feel we need or want. *Therefore, while it is correct to say we are not consumers, it is a grave mistake to say that we are not receivers.*

Generally speaking, when we find church boring or doctrine dead, we tend to complicate matters by turning inward and making ourselves the primary givers and servers in the church service. Instead of returning to what made it exciting in the first place—the greatest rescue story ever told—we try to create our own excitements. We want to find the solution in our deeds, our experience or our knowledge. The one place where God promises to graciously descend to serve us for our salvation and refreshment then gets turned into our service. Instead, we should simply refocus our eyes upon Jesus and the gifts he is distributing in this Divine drama. Ironically, it is then and only then that we can actually properly give, i.e., serve. But it's not God who needs our tangible service, it's our neighbor! Rejuvenated by God's service to us we are freed to spend the whole week loving and serving our neighbor. Martin Luther is very helpful here as he distinguished between the passive righteousness we receive from God in our vertical relationship with him and the active righteousness we exhibit in our horizontal relationships with our neighbor. This active righteousness flows out of and does not contribute to the passive righteousness we receive from God. We do serve the Lord (Ps 100:2); however, as Luther pointed out, particularly with respect to the monastics, when we try to appease God, who doesn't need our service, with our good works, he is not impressed. Moreover, we are frustrated, and the needs of our neighbors, who do need our service, are not met. Luther observed that once we are justified before God, there is no place for our good works to go, except out to our neighbors. As an example, apart from the possible legitimate reasons for hand-raising worship generally, such as responsive praise and adoration, people today are often engaging in it to attempt to "connect" themselves with God. This we need not, should not and cannot do. It is God who serves us by connecting with us, not the other way around. Imagine if all that hand raising energy which is expended were diverted to people putting their arms around their spouses, their children and extending genuine hands of friendship to the visitors beyond a perfunctory greeting!

We have somehow succeeded in turning God's service to us on its head. If there is anything that needs reforming in the contemporary church's worship service, this is it. In order to do this, ministers need to recover their functions as waiters or under-shepherds whose job it is to feed the flock. Their job is not CEO, life coach, salesman, comedian, guru, or motivational speaker. Further, sheep are best led by being called, not by being driven from behind and beaten over the head. Parishioners need to come to receive the kingdom he is bringing, even now in the forgiveness of sins, and then to herald it, not to attempt to build it. Harking back to their own historic tradition, many Reformed churches today are recovering this sense of worship and again calling their services the Divine Service, like the Lutherans have continued to do.

We need to rest in his promises that he will accomplish his purposes through the means of grace (Word and Sacrament) that he has ordained. Like Abraham sleeping with Hagar instead of Sarah, we want to "help" God get things done through our own "effective" means. He has already ordained salvation for a multitude which no one can number. *He is accomplishing his purposes through means that, like Sarah's old and barren womb, look not only weak and foolish to us, but impossible!* He is not only the object of worship, but the subject as well. He was, and is, and ever will be, the primary actor. His promises are sure and powerfully effectual. We are all but beggars when we assemble in his name.

2

The Law-Gospel Distinction

THE DISTINCTION BETWEEN THE law and the gospel is another central truth that has all but been lost over the years. Reformers Martin Luther and John Calvin, as well as others, such as William Tyndale, Theodore Beza, and Charles Spurgeon to name a few, all basically maintained that anyone who did not understand this distinction did not understand the Bible. So what is it? The idea is that God speaks to us in his word with two types of words, law and gospel. Ken Jones, echoing both the Heidelberg Catechism and Book of Concord, broadly defines it as the law being everything that God requires of us and the gospel being everything that God gives to us. Further, what he graciously gives to us "in the gospel, is everything that he has demanded in the law."[1] The law essentially consists of the righteous requirements of our holy Creator God, given for our good, the standards of which we cannot meet. This is due to the unholy state we find ourselves in, which resulted from Adam's fall. Humanity, as his progeny, was plunged into a sinful condition, subject to a state of spiritual death and to physical death along with him. The gospel, which we will examine more fully below, is essentially the good news of God, the Father sending his Son, Jesus Christ, anointed by the Holy Spirit, on a rescue mission to deliver his children and all creation from this predicament. In accomplishing this mission, Christ forgives sins through his atoning death on the cross. Uniting us to himself, he also imputes his righteousness to believers through his perfectly lived life, earning for us, eternal life and the renewal of all things.

1. Jones, "Rightly Dividing the Word."

Part 1: Rediscovering Some Foundational Biblical Truths

The resulting benefits of the new birth, justification, adoption, sanctification, resurrection, and glorification to eternal life are applied to individuals throughout history by the work of the Holy Spirit. Learning to "rightly divide the Word" largely has to do with being able to discern when the Bible is speaking law, i.e., the commands to do or not to do something, and when it is speaking gospel, i.e., the good news and who Christians are "in Christ" as a result of that good news. Much of the legalism present in churches, both yesterday and today, largely results from a failure to properly distinguish between law and gospel.

There are many words we could use to describe the distinction at hand beside gospel and law: indicative and imperative, covenants of grace and covenants of works, promise and purpose, grace and duty, receiving and doing, gift and wage, Abrahamic covenant and Mosaic covenant, Mt. Zion and Mt. Sinai, and, inheritance and employment contract. The Bible uses the language of ancient Near East covenants throughout. Even if you know nothing about ancient Near East covenants and the covenants in the Bible, it is crucial to understand that the new covenant and God's promise of bringing us to the new "Zion" is a continuation of the Abrahamic covenant which is a unilateral covenant of grace like a will. It is not like the Mosaic covenant at Sinai which was a conditional covenant of works that the Israelites had to obey if they wished to remain in the promised land. The Sinai covenant was more like an employment contract. (To be sure, there is also much grace in being given a very undeserved employment contract; however; the operative principle or focus of this covenant was the condition of Israel having to be obedient in order to remain in the promised land.) As Christians we are under the new covenant which is not like an employment contract, but like a last will and testament where we are simply beneficiaries. The Bible, both Old and New Testaments, will be very confusing at places, if this basic distinction is not understood.

Similarly, by nature we tend to flip to the second half of the New Testament epistles when scanning for a passage to read from the Bible. The reason for this is that generally the first halves of the epistles contain indicatives—who we are in Christ, i.e., gospel good news. The second half contains the imperatives—the to-do lists, i.e., the law which we naturally incline toward. By nature we love the law and gravitate toward it, though, being sinful, we distort it. Then, once we have defined the law the way we would like, we turn around and are often prone to call it the gospel. Consider how many titles of Christian bestsellers emphasize the law over the gospel: *The*

The Law-Gospel Distinction

Purpose Driven Life, Become a Better You, My Utmost for His Highest, Radical, Follow Me, Be Mature, Be Confident, and so on. There is not necessarily anything wrong, *per se*, with any of these titles. The problem is that where we put such an emphasis on the law, the gospel is often assumed and then lost. (To his credit, John Bunyan saw fit to write "Justification: A Defense of the Doctrine of Justification" before he went on to pen *Pilgrim's Progress*.) In pursuing the implications of the gospel, the goal should never be to move beyond the gospel, "but to move us more deeply into it."[2]

Even sections of the Bible that are primarily gospel are often read by us as if they were primarily law. One example is the Beatitudes in Matthew 5. Understanding them primarily, not as a list of conditional rules, but as covenant blessings being given out by the covenant mediator, makes a huge difference. These ought always to be read in their context as descriptive, declarative utterances of Jesus: there are simply no "ifs" in them.

Likewise, church services today often offer nothing more than good tips for living and that is held out as the good news! By nature we like the practical. The problem is that while the law is good and gives us guidance, it is powerless to actually change us. In trying to motivate changes in behavior, many preachers today are simply beating their congregants over the head, week after week, with one exhortation after another. *They are trying to accomplish with the law something that only the gospel can ultimately do.* The nature of the gospel is completely different than that of the law. It is a gracious announcement of good news. The gospel consists of statements of fact about something which has already happened in history. In fact, it is such good news and filled with such Divine power, that it is precisely what actually has transforming power. But that notion is counterintuitive to us. Instead of heralding this gospel, we have turned it on its head similar to the Divine Service. When we talk about the gospel now, we talk about being the gospel or living the gospel which is a total confusion of categories.[3] May God have mercy if the gospel is not about him, but about me! Of course there is a place to talk about obedience, but that is a different category. It consists of living in light of the good news of the gospel.

---

2. Tchividjian, *One Way Love*, 213.
3. See Horton, "Missional Church or New Monasticism?," 17.

3

Easy as 1-2-3 vs. Just Shoot Me Now

So how do we live in light of the gospel? Once we understand the distinction between the law and the gospel, we come to what the Reformers defined as the three uses of the law as it relates to the ongoing use of the gospel. When Herman Cain ran for president in the 2012 Republican primary he had a slogan, "999," which he used to define his message at every campaign stop. Every time you saw Herman Cain, you heard him saying 999 and describing his proposed policies represented by those numbers. Christians similarly again need to assimilate into their very beings a "1-2-3" concerning the three uses of the law, on a daily basis as did the apostles and the Reformers. The 1-2-3 that we are referring to is *not* reciting the three uses of the law, i.e., law, law, law—which is what we are prone to do. People often end up talking about the three uses of the law in isolation from the gospel which has created, and which continues to create, all kinds of mischief. While there are three uses of the law, it is probably better to speak in terms of the "law/gospel 1-2-3" so that the law does not become isolated from the gospel. Therefore, as we will see, the 1-2-3 goes like this: the first (crushing) use of the law, followed by the second ongoing use of the gospel, followed by the third descriptive use of the law, i.e., law, gospel, law. The law which indicts, prosecutes, and convicts us is followed by the gospel which acquits and liberates us which is followed by the law of love, the law of freedom. Every time we hear an imperative, something we must do, we should immediately go to this 1-2-3 process so that it becomes ingrained in our thinking as a way of life. How so?

Easy as 1-2-3 vs. Just Shoot Me Now

The first use of the law is to crush us and kill us and send us running to the Savior. We must understand that every time we hear a "to do" from God, woe are we. We cannot possibly ever keep the law perfectly and do what God requires in the light of his absolute holiness. And the laws he gives us will do that. For instance, he tells us to be perfect (Matt 5:48). He tells us that our righteousness must exceed that of the scribes and Pharisees (Matt 5:20). We simply cannot meet the standards of his holiness this side of heaven. Every human being is born with a corrupt nature before God. While a lot of people may be nice and exhibit a civic righteousness, this is not about how we perceive one another. With a holy God, the standards are incomprehensibly different. Scripture reveals that no human being can stand in the blazing light of his holiness (e.g., Rom 3:9–20). Ultimately a mediator is needed to rescue us. This is what God graciously provides in the person and work of his Son, Jesus Christ. Far from leaving us to languish in our crushed state (which is what some churches have been known to do), the first use of the law should immediately lead us to what we are calling the "use" of the gospel for both the believer and unbeliever. The good news of the gospel is not only that Jesus died for my sins but also lived a perfectly obedient life in my place as well. This is so important because my status as a Christian is not simply a return to Adam in the garden of Eden or to Israel in the promised land, but the imputation to me of his active obedience earning for me my right to eat of the tree of life and enjoy everlasting Sabbath rest in a new heavens and earth, i.e., the resurrection of the body and the life everlasting.

What we like to do is to lower the bar and preach laws we can actually keep for a time. Instead of continually killing the old Adam and continually nourishing our new life in Christ, our tendency is to try and improve the old Adam. The Reformers saw the importance of this distinction. This process was referred to as mortification and vivification: the continuous dying to our sinful nature and the continuous bringing to life of our new nature by virtue of our union with Christ. This is why the indicative of who we are "in Christ" is so important, not just for our justification, but for our sanctification as well.

The second use of the law is not as relevant for our purposes. It is simply the recognition that law also has a general civil purpose in society both for Christians and non-Christians. There are certain basic norms required for peaceful living in any civilization. Some sins are more than sins; they are also crimes (or traffic violations) which create a debt to society in addition to one's debt to God. Thus, when it comes to crimes, even where there is forgiveness by God and even by the victim, there is still a legitimate penalty to the civil authorities that must be satisfied. So the second use of the law simply serves as a check to see if any of my sins also constitute any type of civil infraction and, if so, to recognize the legitimate civil penalty that must be paid.

The third use of the law for the Christian, is that it directs or guides our gratitude toward God and our love for neighbor. Because of the first use of the law, I immediately run to Jesus and find my safety there. Mt. Sinai no longer thunders at me and I am free in Christ to obey, not out of fear of punishment or hope of earning reward, but simply out of gratitude and love because I am united to his perfect obedience already accomplished for me. For the first time I can actually see a small beginning of real obedience because my motives are being purified. Not that we are perfect yet, but we do see an "already" aspect of our redemption beginning in this age of the "not yet." There is a real change in motive and the impurities still present in our best motives are also cleansed on account of Christ. The Reformers had correctly identified three biblical elements for a work to truly constitute a good work before God: (1) conforms to the law of God; (2) proceeds from faith in Jesus Christ; and (3) is done to the glory of God. Works done with a motive to save ourselves or to put feathers in our caps represent nothing more than self-love and therefore are ultimately not good works at all.

By nature, we think we can be promise keepers and pull it off ourselves. We continuously say what Israel said at Mt. Sinai: "All that the LORD has spoken we will do, and we will be obedient" (Exod 24:7). The problem is that using the law to improve our old Adam will ultimately never work. It will either lead to self-righteous Pharisaism, a.k.a. legalism or moralism, or, on the other hand, to despair. This is largely what ails the church today. We have gone from a stern, heavy legalism (don't do this or you will go to hell) to a smiley, lighter, form of legalism (do this and you will be happy). Since the law kills and can never give life, even living under this newer lighter form of legalism is like a nagging, infectious toothache leading to a slow death. Many end up in despair, expressing the sentiment of the popular quip "just shoot me now."

So how does the 1-2-3 work? Every time I come across a command of God, something I ought to do or not do, I must immediately recognize that in this life I am simultaneously saint and sinner and cannot and have not kept this requirement perfectly. Rather than sit there with a stricken conscience and have Mt. Sinai thunder at me, I immediately shoot my old Adam, run to Christ and find my liberating comfort in his active obedience on my behalf (the second ongoing use of the gospel). Then, drawing upon my union with Christ, I go to the third use of the law and in view of the mercies of God, free in Christ, offer myself as a living sacrifice of love and thanksgiving, guided by the law with a clean conscience. Again and again, I must return to this 1-2-3 pattern of thought. Often we can lose the first use of the law (and thereby the ongoing use of the gospel) by assuming it in much the same way as people lose the gospel by it being assumed after they become Christians and are subsequently given nothing but law. There is no more of a gracious Lutheran toward the Calvinists than Dr. Rod Rosenbladt. Nonetheless, he has astutely pointed out that many Reformed Calvinists have had a tendency to stay so focused on the third use of the law that it eventually gobbles up the first use. When that happens you find yourself in the same legalistic bondage as those who are trying to improve the old Adam under the law. The third use of the law then comes accompanied by carrots and/or sticks as motivators and Christians are put back on an endless treadmill.

Law and gospel must always be read together. Specifically, the three uses of the law must always be read in conjunction with the ongoing use of the gospel. Like the law, the gospel has many uses as well. We could say that the first use of the gospel, i.e., the first time we are drawn to it by the first use of the law is for our justification. The second ongoing use of the gospel is the never-ending nourishment for the Christian and his or her sanctification—increasingly dying to sin and increasingly coming alive in Christ. It alone is what will properly motivate and propel the Christian in the third use of the law. Think, for instance, of the "double cure"[1] reference to the gospel in the hymn "Rock of Ages, Cleft for Me." The third use of the law is just a guide or description. Such exhortations can only give direction. Carrots and sticks might have some superficial effect, but they will not change you from the inside out. Only the ongoing use of the gospel will do that and produce affections for God's law.

Therefore, when I read that I must be perfect, rather than becoming spiritually anorexic,[2] I first run to Christ and know that through my union with him I am reckoned as perfect before the Father and then I move on with a renewed obedience. When I read I am to lay up for myself treasures in

---

1. Augustus M. Toplady, "Rock of Ages, Cleft for Me," in *Psalter Hymnal*, no. 388.
2. See Maas, "On Being Well-Dressed," 17.

heaven, I again first run to Christ and look at how he has already fulfilled that on my behalf (Col 1:3–5). The same goes for being humble, being a good spouse and every other command in Scripture.

Often in Scripture, where the context concerns those who would presume to justify themselves before God by the keeping of the law, Jesus purposely states the law in an over-the-top, crushing sort of way (e.g., with the Pharisees listening in, "you must be perfect," and "your righteousness must exceed that of the Pharisees," or to the rich young ruler, "sell everything and give to the poor," or to the lawyer in the parable of the Good Samaritan, "go, and do likewise.") It is very important in such settings to read the law in context and recognize its function to crush hardened hearts. By plowing hard, the soil of the hard heart can be softened for planting the seed of the gospel in the broken-hearted. As we will see later, *what the rich young ruler and the lawyer were asked to do is what Jesus actually did for us! These stories first point us to him who fulfilled all righteousness.* At the same time, there is a sweetness for the already brokenhearted in the third use of the law, where the law is not only defanged of all its venom, but, like a puppy, becomes man's best friend. Perfection, generosity and love for enemy, all illustrated in these stories and teachings of Jesus, become wonderful guideposts to light our way.

Even being exposed to the wonderful Reformational teachings which are the essence of this book, including law and gospel and the proper uses of the law, can be turned into all law. This can make one neurotic, i.e., neurotic about the many "diluted" Christian teachings that make people neurotic and how I must fix it for family, friends and others. Even here I must learn to rest in him. He is the Savior, not me. There is one perfect teacher. "There's one good Father and one good Son"[3]—and it isn't me! That I might now apprehend more of the truth (which has been there all along whether I realized it or not) doesn't mean I'm now going to save that part of the world in which I find myself (a "just shoot me now" heavy burden of law). It means that I should see, even more, my need for the Lord to have mercy on me, a sinner (first use of the law) and recognize that he will be the perfect teacher, father and son and thereby I apprehend more of his love (ongoing use of the gospel). Then by his grace, out of a grateful heart, I can therefore begin to testify of his grace and mercy in thought, word and deed (third use of the law as guide for direction without the crushing burden). His yoke is easy and his burden is light (Matt 11:29–30). To apprehend his love

---

3. Fitzpatrick, "Parenting with Discipline and Grace."

is amazing. To apprehend his truth without apprehending his sovereign love can be crushing. By nature I worry if family and friends will ever truly appreciate these priceless biblical treasures recovered in the Reformation and by nature I want to fix it. Yet in my own case, I was born in it and yet squandered some of, or at least was far too lazy and ambivalent about, the riches of the Reformation that my parents sought to pass down to me. Who could have ever imagined the unlikely people that God would eventually use to become mentors to me (and many others) to help fill in the gaps with the riches of orthodox Protestant Reformation Christianity? The fears and worries that the law produces in me, due to my sinful nature, are never necessary. Again, it is God's gospel promises that are sure and certain, no matter how precarious or hopeless things might look to us.

4

The Gospel Is Objective and Powerful

So exactly what is this good news that we call the gospel (a.k.a. the evangel)? In a nutshell, it is that two thousand years ago, in a particular place, God sent his Son to live a perfectly obedient life, die for our sins on the cross, and be raised for our justification. This short version is summarized in 1 Corinthians 15 which includes the historical fact that the resurrected Christ appeared to over five hundred people at one time. Paul's letter to the Corinthians was written early on, probably before AD 60. He basically invites his hearers to check out the truth of his story, reminding them that most of those five hundred people were still alive around the vicinity of Jerusalem. The gospel is the culmination of God working through centuries of history to fulfill his promise of redemption for his children and the entire creation at great personal cost to himself. This promise of redemption was first made to Adam and Eve after the fall in Genesis 3:15 and then more specifically to Abraham and Sarah later in Genesis 12 and 15. It was centered in the promised seed, the Messiah, meaning Savior. The gospel also includes the promise of his second advent when he will come in glory to fully consummate his redemptive plan, raise the dead to life everlasting and usher in the new heavens and earth. The apostles, who were initially cowards before Jesus' resurrection and Pentecost, ended up going to the ends of the then known world to tell this gospel (good news) and were willing to die for doing so.[1]

---

1. Some balk at the lack of a universal salvation in Christianity; however, would we really obligate God to save every Adolf Hitler at such a great cost? Given the sinful,

The Gospel Is Objective and Powerful

The gospel was and is the testimony concerning these facts. It is objective and outside of me. It is not my personal testimony of my inner, subjective experience of how I feel or how I once felt. Of course the gospel produces a variety of positive subjective experiences to which many appropriately testify to. Experiences, however, can come and go. While my personal testimonial may or may not be interesting to others, it is not the gospel. It may be the result of the gospel, but it is not the gospel. In American pop evangelicalism, those who are not raised as Christians (or who have rebelled from a Christian upbringing) and then have a sudden conversion experience have often tended to equate the subjective effects that they feel with the gospel itself. While often less knowledgeable, they usually are more zealous in their faith than those raised in the faith and, consequently, often tend to be elevated to positions of leadership in the church. They invariably then have a very difficult time relating to those nurtured in the faith since infancy, particularly their own children, when they grew up in the desert before coming to the oasis. It is very hard for a person with that type of experience, who has conflated that experience with the good news, to understand the experience of one growing up in the oasis of the church. Instead of letting the real gospel do its work, they perpetually try to project their experience on the younger ones growing up in the church. Many growing up under this tyranny have had the same experience of feeling compelled to "ask Jesus into your heart" thousands of times, trying to make the earth shake for themselves. The reality is that children who grow up in a Christian environment often have a subjective experience that is the converse. While often they will not testify to any sudden dramatic change in their own subjective, inner feelings, they are often stunned at the dry wasteland and empty void they find in many people's lives in their initial ventures outside the covenant community (i.e., the visible church).

We have lost the ordinary means God uses to nurture his covenant children, i.e., children born to families already in the church. *The important thing is not about being able to recall or describe your spiritual birth, it is to know that you are alive.* Instead of only looking for sudden "born-again" conversion experiences, *a common norm for children growing up in the church ought to be that they can't remember a time when Jesus was not sweet to their lips, nor a time when they were not turning to him for the forgiveness of their sins.* God is much more gracious than we give him credit for.

---

spiritually treasonous state of humanity, the real mystery of God's electing love is not: why are many saved and not others? The real mystery is: why any?

He does not implement a universal plan to routinely adopt sinners as his own children and then give these children a bunch of unregenerates for children, only so that the parents can nervously hope for a much later high school or college age sudden conversion. Evangelicals with this mindset usually then look for such a conversion at some event or camp outside all of the nurturing that took place in the church and home![2] He is much more gracious than that. The general intent as revealed in Scripture is that God will graciously work in the hearts of the lambs of his sheep from a young age as they participate in being nurtured through Word and Sacrament. How could this be when they understand so little?

The gospel is not only objective, it is powerful. Paul tells us it is the power unto salvation (Rom 1:16). Peter similarly writes, "Since you have been born again, not of perishable seed but of imperishable, through the living and abiding word of God . . . and this word is the good news that was preached to you (1 Pet 1: 23–25). Likewise, John writes, "See what kind of love the Father has given to us that we should be called children of God; and so we are" (1 John 3:1). This is further vividly foreshadowed in the OT with Ezekiel's vision of a valley of skeletons coming to life simply through his preaching (Ezek 37). While the law kills, the gospel brings life. The gospel is in the nature of a promise, a promise of God. *Its very announcement brings about the reality of which it speaks. It is not merely advisory. It is not merely teaching. It has a sacramental quality to it.* Though that word may sound Roman Catholic to many pop evangelical ears, it is thoroughly biblical when properly understood. "Faith comes from hearing, and hearing through the word of Christ" (Rom 10:17).

The analogies Scripture uses to illustrate our regeneration make this abundantly clear. It is like when God said, "Let there be light," and there was light. He didn't say let there be a possibility of light if the light would so choose. Similarly, Scripture says believers are a new creation by the power of his Word (2 Cor 5:17; Gal 6:15). Likewise, it was by the power of his word that Jesus raised Lazarus from the dead. Again, we were "dead in our sins" and have been raised "in newness of life" (Eph 2; Rom 5–6).

While Lutherans and the Reformed/Presbyterians/Anglicans have some differences in their understanding of the sacraments, they all recognize the sacramental nature of both God's Word and the visible signs he uses to seal his promises in baptism and the Lord's Supper. Contrary to the Roman Catholic view that the sacraments are automatically effectual

2. See Horton, *Gospel Commission*, 174.

simply by their being performed by the church, irrespective of the presence of faith, the Reformation properly understood them as means of grace made effectual when received through faith, which is also a mysteriously bestowed gift of God.

The Reformers properly understood regeneration or being "born again" as God's miracle enabling one's faith rather than one's faith decision enabling God's miracle. While both Calvinist and Lutheran theology is characterized by the former, many of today's pop evangelicals have succumbed to the latter, which was taught by Jacobus Arminius and later popularized by John Wesley. *While the Reformers acknowledged humanity's free will in countless areas, when it came to connecting with or making oneself right with God, this was something that humans were no more capable of than jumping to the moon.* The spiritually dead had to first be born again, or born from above, and being born is passive. Some pop evangelicals have gone even further than the Arminian teaching (sometimes called decisional regeneration) which at least acknowledges that man needs the Holy Spirit's assistance for him to cooperate with and thereby "make a decision" (and so jump to the moon). Pelagianism, named after a fourth-century monk named Pelagius, leaves it solely within the ability of man. While Reformational evangelicals regard Arminianism as a serious mistake and a failure to fully appreciate the extent of God's gracious work, the church overall has long regarded Pelagianism (complete do-it-yourself-ism) as a heresy, i.e., a foundational error. Contrary to a popular misunderstanding of the Reformation doctrine of election, there is no such thing as someone wanting in, but not being able to get in because their name is not on the list. Properly understood, election recognizes that anyone who wants in on believing in Christ, is in and will do so.

While word and sacrament gospel proclamation and administration is officially the job of ministers of established churches and of missionaries planting new churches, all Christians, whatever their calling, ought to, in some way, also be part of the effort. Christians are citizens of two kingdoms. Not all Christians should pretend to hold the office of missionary, but all Christians do have the privilege of being evangelical, always prepared to give the reason for their hope. Christians should be zealous to see that this gospel, this evangel, is widely proclaimed, both to themselves and to others. The proclamation of the gospel is, after all, the ordinary means God has decided to use to create and sustain faith by the power of the Holy Spirit.

5

The Gospel
More than We Could Ever Hope for or Imagine

WHILE THE HEART OF the gospel is that nugget described above, a vast array of benefits accompany it as well. Therefore, the gospel can also more broadly refer to all the good news which flows from it, particularly as we distinguish law and gospel. While increasingly the gospel today is confused with law, i.e., as in "living the gospel," the pop evangelicals who have maintained the proper law-gospel distinction, have so twisted and limited the good news that, even then, it is barely recognizable as good news. What passes today for presenting the gospel is but a distorted fraction of the greatest story ever told. At best, the gospel today is often presented as merely an entrance way into the kingdom of heaven. It is just a doorway by which ones escapes the threat of hell at death. Even the doorway itself is usually distorted. It is viewed as the door to one's heart through which Jesus must pass and enter in. Hence, as we seen, reference is often made to "inviting Jesus into your heart." Moreover, pop evangelicals contend that it is you who must open this door. Put another way, Jesus is the lifeguard who throws the life preserver about 99 percent your way and you must swim that other 1 percent toward him and take hold. Finally, once Jesus is in your heart, you've got your ticket to heaven and now it is all about you living the Christian life and seeking his favor by your obedience and your efforts to live a life of radical discipleship.

This picture is wrong in so many ways. First, we must understand that it is not about me—even a little bit. It surely is for me, but it is not about me. As we have seen, the good news is the story about Jesus' life, death and resurrection for my justification before God. It concerns what he has done and what he continues to do in applying the benefits of his finished work. It carries with it innumerable gifts. As one hymn writer put it: "How vast the benefits Divine, which we in Christ possess"![1] The implications of this good news are enormous. It remains relevant as much for Christians as it is for the yet unbelieving. It is a not just a once-upon-a-time story, but a story that keeps giving and giving and giving. *Its saving benefits continue to flow from its retelling. It is a never-ending wellspring of cleansing, reclothing, and nourishing.* Every telling of the gospel is another occasion to hear more of the Father's last will and testament being read and what he has provided, is providing and will provide for his adopted children. He not only accomplished everything for my salvation, but ensures its effective delivery to me as well. The doorway into God's kingdom is only the beginning of the good news, not the end. Christ himself is our *telos*, the end of all things.

Moreover, the doorway itself is the opposite from that usually presented. Primarily, it is not Christ that needs to be relocated in me, but the other way around. By nature, I am in Adam. "I am the one, rather than Jesus, who needs to be relocated!"[2] I need to be found, heart, soul, strength and mind, in Christ. "Inviting Jesus into your heart" is simply nowhere to be found in Scripture. The often-cited verse "Behold, I stand at the door and knock" (Rev 3:20) is not addressed to my heart, but to a church that has abandoned Christ. To be sure, we are, by the Holy Spirit, mystically united with the presence of Christ who is seated at the right hand of the Father. In that sense it is said that Christ dwells in and with us, applying his benefits to us. Primarily, though, it is me who first needs to be relocated into Christ as he is our heavenly advocate who pleads our cause before the Father. Moreover, that relocation is not the expression of a vague feeling of accepting Jesus to be my invisible friend. It is very specifically repenting, being baptized, and receiving the gifts of new life and faith—not faith in faith, but faith in the person and work of Jesus. The Reformers carefully defined faith as consisting of knowledge of the basic gospel of Christ and his work, assent to these facts as true, and personal trust in Christ and his saving work for oneself. (While this what many people do mean when they

---

1. Augustus M. Toplady, "How Vast the Benefits Divine," rev. by Dewey Westra, in *Psalter Hymnal*, no. 386.
2. Horton, *Gospel-Driven Life*, 92.

refer to inviting Jesus into their heart, such a shorthand saying unbiblically and dangerously distorts the picture.)

Furthermore, Jesus is the Savior, not just a helper to get you relocated there. Jesus is not a wimp who merely makes salvation possible. *He is not helplessly standing at the door of your heart begging for you to let him in.* He regenerates those who are dead in sin and makes them alive with new affections and the gift of faith so that you will believe and be found in him. He is not the helpless lifeguard on the shore just making our rescue possible by throwing out the life preserver and now pleading with you to save yourself. *He is the lifeguard that dives a mile down to the ocean floor rescuing our spiritually dead selves. His Spirit locks lips with our treasonous mouths breathing new life and faith into us.* If the Bible could be summed up in a verse, it would be a verse such as: "Salvation belongs to the Lord" (Jonah 2:9), or, "For from him and through him and to him are all things" (Rom 11:36), or, "Jesus, the founder and perfector of our faith" (Heb 12:2).

Even more than that, we are not merely brought back to Adam and Eve's position before God prior to the Fall. Christ further fulfilled the covenant of works on our behalf earning our eternal Sabbath rest and the right to eat from the tree of life. Adam, as well as the nation of Israel, were given tests to perform. If Adam passed the test, drove the serpent from the garden, as he should have, and lived in full faith and obedience, he would be rewarded with that eternal Sabbath rest, eating from the Tree of Life. If he failed, death would come to him and his progeny, i.e., us. Israel was similarly a model of God's kingdom. While they simultaneously enjoyed covenants of grace with God for their and our ultimate salvation, insofar as their remaining in the promised land was concerned, they were, like Adam, also under a covenant of works. If they passed that test, drove God's enemies out completely in faith and obedience, they would similarly be rewarded with long life in the land. If they failed, they would be exiled from the land.

"But like Adam, they transgressed the covenant" (Hos 6:7). Scripture here explicitly tells us they were both under a covenant of works and both failed. Jesus then comes as the second Adam for the express purpose of fulfilling all righteousness (Matt 3:15; 5:17). He spends forty days in the wilderness where he is tempted by the devil. Unlike Adam and Israel, he sends the sends the devil fleeing and continues to live a perfectly obedient life. This is what is referred to as Jesus active obedience. Under the new covenant of grace, this obedience is imputed to those who are in Christ by virtue of their union with Christ. Since we have this wonderful covenant mediator, God the Father sees us "in Christ" as we have alluded to earlier. This is our new identity. It is who we are now before God, despite our remaining sinful condition.

To use a scoring analogy, Adam basically started out at 0 percent. He could have scored 100 percent on the test. He failed and brought us all down to minus 100 percent. In Christ we are not merely brought back to 0 percent with having to prove ourselves to him by earning his favor, which is the prevailing model in pop evangelicalism. In Christ we are brought up to 100 percent. *We are not only restored from our indebtedness, but positively blessed with the merits of Christ.* (This language "through the merits of [Christ]" is often used in the prayers in the Anglican Book of Common Prayer and other old Reformation prayers as well.) Therefore, even as we presently remain in a condition where sin is still present, "there is therefore now no condemnation for those who are in Christ Jesus" (Rom 8:1). He has seated us in the heavenly places with Christ. As an aside, this is at least partly why Jesus gives such crushing law to those who would presume to save themselves. If Adam didn't do it starting with a clean slate at 0 percent, could the rich young ruler or the lawyer in the Good Samaritan story ever be able to truly love and thereby "save" their neighbors, or even themselves, when they themselves and their neighbors were starting with sinful natures at minus 100 percent!

Does this amazing grace mean that we will now live out our lives encouraged to sin all the more? Will this free grace cause a proliferation of alcohol abuse, adultery, and a lack of concern for world hunger? (Rom 6). No—and this is another missing ingredient of the pop version of the gospel—*the gospel is the power not just for our justification, but for our actual sanctification as well.* As we alluded to earlier, it is the nourishing fuel for living the Christian life. It's even more gift. "He who began a good work in you will bring it to completion at the day of Jesus Christ" (Phil 1:6). He gives to our hearts new affections. Understanding and basking in the good news that we are free in Christ because we are united to him and his active obedience on our behalf is crucial. Our consciences are then free from all condemnation and we can begin to obey without self-interest as we no longer need to save ourselves or earn our reward. "Obedience is no route to the blessings of fellowship with him. Rather, obedience itself is a blessing of our fellowship and union with Christ, and a result of the principle of new life which his Spirit has implanted in us."[3] We don't obey for the blessing, we understand that our new obedience is part of the blessing. We love from salvation, not for salvation.[4] Our salvation has already been secured. Our reward is already secured for us in our inheritance. Our motives, and therefore our works, in loving and serving our neighbors, become sanctified. Our very best works, which are as filthy rags in his holy sight, are purified through the merits of Christ. This is what growing in the grace and knowledge of Christ is all about. Tullian Tchividjian has repeatedly observed that grace does not create licentiousness, but legalism does. If a tree had a mind, its focus would primarily be on the sun shining on its leaves and the soil by its roots. The focus would be on where to get its nourishment, not on its fruit. The branches' producing and being fruitful would then eventually and naturally take care of itself. *Sinking our roots in his radical person and work and being illumined by the Holy Spirit are what will richly yield the fruit of faith, not our self- absorbed focusing on our radical efforts to justify our existence as branches.*

And the story keeps on giving and giving. The war is over and there is peace. There is our adoption as children of the Heavenly Father. There is the inheritance. There is the resurrection and glorification of our bodies. There is the new heavens and the new earth. There is the life everlasting. There is the ecstasy of a perfectly consummated marriage. There is the great homecoming where we will bask in the everlasting presence of Father, Son and Spirit. We cannot even begin to fathom all of the benefits which those in Christ possess. Far from being an tiresome old story, there is no end to the glorious gifts given to us in the gospel!

---

3. Lee, "Why We Seek to Know God's Will," 33.
4. See Tchividjian, *One Way Love*, 189.

PART 2

How We Do Church
The Contemporary Protestant Evangelical Church Service and the Need for Reform

6

For Members Only . . . Not

HAVING ESTABLISHED SOME FOUNDATIONAL principles, we now turn to the local church and the typical service we find inside. While the majority of issues addressed in this volume pertain to the more contemporary expressions of evangelical Christianity, this one is for the traditionalists. It's always amazing to observe how often the layout of a church facility appears to have been designed not to bring people in, but to keep them out. Sometimes churches were built hidden in the woods off of a side street—and this was before the days of GPS! Often the main entrance of the church was really just for show as the parking lot was invariably in the back where there would be a "secret" entrance which the members actually used. A visitor could never be expected to use this "members" entrance that everyone else was using. Many of these churches were simply, by design, not very visitor friendly. The Great Commission was, in part, correctly viewed as a mandate to establish new churches; however, once established, churches often were incorrectly viewed as limited to passing on the faith from generation to generation and not "for all who are far off" in their own neighborhoods (Acts 2:39). Churches often ended up functioning like private clubs. To be sure, church membership is important, but visitors should always be welcome.

The assumption that only members would use such an innocuous door has long been deeply ingrained in our society. While I was attending college in the hometown of the president of the United States, the president came to town for a weekend campaign visit. My roommate and I had heard the president would be attending his home church just up the street from us and thought it would be a fun idea to go with him. When we were a block away from the church we realized a lot of other people had the same idea. We spotted a large crowd and the media near the front door of the church in taped off areas. Having been raised in traditional churches, we both instinctively knew that if we just acted like members we would be okay. So we nonchalantly kept walking toward the "secret" side door where the actual church members were trickling in. Sure enough, we smiled a good morning to multiple secret service agents both at the door and inside and proceeded to sit a couple of rows behind the president and his family.

On another occasion I was visiting a former church where some years earlier I had served on the council. Now, in entering this church, you had to pick your poison. You had two choices. There was an entrance that most of the members used. The only problem was that it was a side entrance to the sanctuary which meant that everyone seated there could (and would) watch everyone coming in. Wanting to be more discreet on this particular visit, I opted for the other (main) entrance in the rear. As I approached the large gothic type doors which were seldom used, I felt a certain terror entering this place—and this was a place with which I was all too familiar, having stood in the front on several occasions to offer a prayer or make an announcement. I could only imagine how a real visitor might feel. To be sure, such a feeling is not at all inappropriate in approaching God in his sanctuary, who is described as a consuming fire, and, who is to be worshipped in reverence and awe (Heb 12:28). Noted Presbyterian pastor, author, and Reformation Study Bible editor R. C. Sproul makes this important point in his classic book *The Holiness of God*.[1] But even the Old Testament temple proper was surrounded with both an approachable, welcoming outer Jewish court and a Gentile court for the people outside of the covenant community! God's gracious design provided that one didn't stumble into the holy of holies, when entering the temple!

This is one area where the contemporary church marketing movement can be commended to some extent. It's not that the church sanctuaries themselves should be redesigned as many are prone to do; it's about having an appropriate welcoming area outside of the sanctuary. Entrance areas to modern churches are being explicitly designed to welcome any visitors who might wander in. Large open areas with coffee bars are greeting everyone in love and hospitality, replacing the old notion of coffee "in the basement"

---

1. Sproul, *Holiness of God*, 5.

after the service for those visitors who might have previously dared to descend to the depths. And this is a good thing.

7

Restoring the Elements of Worship

WHILE THE CHURCHES OF the Reformation differed somewhat in how formal and structured the liturgy was to be, they were all agreed, on a basic level, as to what the elements were to a Divine Service. Today's American pop evangelicals have a liturgy of sorts, albeit a very simple one. Usually the service begins with someone saying good morning and then Jesus being invited with a brief prayer. This is usually followed by a half dozen (usually happy clappy praise) songs led in pop/rock entertainment style by a band on a stage. This is usually then followed by an offering accompanied by some sort of video and then a message and a dismissal. There might also be some other innovations sprinkled in there such as: skits, puppets, liturgical dance, and giveaways for Mother's Day.

Unfortunately this new model didn't result from merely trying to update the old way of doing things. The contemporary model resulted from a completely different approach, i.e., a marketing approach to church by both by nineteenth-century revivalists and the twentieth-century church growth or marketing movement. Consequently, this new approach discarded many of the elements historically common to the various Reformational denominations as well as the early church.

The historical elements of worship are not based upon a consumer or entertainment model, but rather are based upon the patterns we find in Scripture when God meets with his people. Because the Triune God is present in a special or saving way as opposed to a general presence that we find, for example, in nature, there is a sacramental element in addition to merely a pedagogical or teaching element. God's servant or minister is not merely there to talk about God, but is there as his representative to bring to the people the very words of God in all of their power. Church is not merely a "teaching ministry" about God, but it is a very real meeting with God. He distributes his gifts in this meeting through the ways he has ordained, i.e., the means of grace which are the Word preached and sacraments administered (baptism and the Lord's Supper).

Historically, the service therefore follows a biblical pattern. Without doing an exhaustive analysis of the various historic liturgies, the following will highlight the basics. (Some sample contemporary liturgies are posted at reformationriches.com to assist evangelical churches that wish to recover these basic elements in their services.) We will then examine some of these basic elements in further detail in subsequent sections. As we will see, good liturgy is very interactive. God graciously addresses us and we respond to him. There is a lot of switching between sitting and standing as the service progresses, without doing either one for uncomfortably long periods of time (as is often the case in evangelicalism). With an appreciation as to what is happening in the liturgy, there is an enjoyable and natural flow to it.

The service often begins with an invocation, i.e., calling on the name of the Lord. Who is this Lord? He is the triune God: Father, Son and Holy Spirit. We don't simply come to meet with Jesus. We come to worship the Father through the Son by the power of the Holy Spirit. Jesus said, "But the hour is coming, and is now here, when the true worshippers will worship the Father in spirit and truth, for the Father is seeking such people to worship him" (John 4:23). There is often then a call to worship by God and a greeting of God (as opposed to a mere good morning from a mere human being) which the people stand to receive. Make no mistake about it: there is no question here whose privilege it is to be present, who is doing the inviting and who is the main actor in the service. The call to worship comes from God's Holy Word calling his people to the great privilege of meeting with the King of kings and Lord of lords. It is spoken from his representative, a servant, a minister whose office is manifest by his robe of authority and/or the pulpit behind which he stands. Having called his people, the holy God of the universe, this consuming fire in whose presence no one can stand, greets those gathered. Instead of consuming everyone in his incomprehensible holiness, he amazingly addresses the congregation through his minister with a profound kindness: "Grace . . . mercy . . . and peace . . . be unto you from the God the Father, God the Son and God the Holy Spirit." Wow! He comes with grace—unmerited favor for sinners; with mercy—the undeserved withholding of judgment; and, with peace—declaring the war to be over with those who were formerly at enmity with him and upon whom his favor now rests. Just getting this far was already really good news—joyous news. Responding to the gracious greeting of the triune God, the people would burst into a song of praise, such as, "Praise to the Lord, the Almighty, the King of Creation."

Now, it is true that many traditional ministers and their congregants through the years were not exactly the most "seeker-sensitive." (Actually, they wouldn't use those words. They would probably use the words "visitor friendly," since the Bible reveals to us that it is God who is the seeker and that no one seeks him in and of him or herself [Rom 3:9–19].) In any event, they could have said hello and welcomed the visitors and skeptics with a true evangelical spirit, explaining the rich liturgical drama that was about to unfold and the role of God's ambassador in proclaiming his good news. That would have avoided a lot of misunderstanding. By the same token, like when a waltz starts, there comes a point when the time for explanations and instructions should fall by the wayside so that the dance can actually unfold. For today's evangelical church in this pop culture, however, there's going to have to be a lot of explaining along the way for people to understand and appreciate what's going on, even when just restoring some of these basic elements and without getting "too liturgical." In the past where there was no explanation of the liturgy, the minister was simply perceived by many as hopelessly out of date and irrelevant compared with the hot-shot mega preacher up the street. It is important that an appreciation be nurtured in the average person for the historic elements of worship and the early-century hymns of the church. In the end, they will understand that to be much more significant (and cool) than what Pastor Slick is doing.

Sometimes the Ten Commandments or another expression of the moral law of God is then read. Once in the presence of this holy God and his holy law, the people realize their unworthiness and confess their sins, followed by an assurance of pardon or absolution. Thus the service begins with the first use of the law and the ongoing use of the gospel described above in a corporate context with all of the people gathered together. We can only have the privilege of being in the Father's special saving presence because we have a mediator, namely Christ.

The more historical liturgical churches follow this with the *Kyrie eleison* ("Lord have mercy"), a biblical and historic plea for God's mercy, in recognition that we are totally dependent upon him for every breath we take. It is a prayer made not just for ourselves, but a prayer made for others—for those in the local church, the church at large, and the entire world. The *Kyrie* was originally in Greek and it is often still sung partly in the original language. It thereby also serves as a reminder that we are part of a body of believers extending historically over millennia, to a time even before the split between the Eastern Greek speaking churches and the Western Latin church. This would be followed by a very joyful song bringing glory and praise to God such as "Glory to God in the Highest" which is based upon Luke 2:14 or the song "Worthy Is Christ (the Lamb)" a.k.a. "This Is the Feast of Victory for Our God" which is based upon Revelation 5: 9–14. Again this follows a pattern that is found in Scripture. See, for example, the story of blind Bartemaeus (Mark 10:46–52; Luke 18:35–43).

Many churches following the historic liturgy follow this with readings from the Old and New Testaments and the Gospels. Then the Word is proclaimed by the minister as a servant of God speaking the very words of God as a means of his grace. With his office highlighted like a judge in a courtroom, he is clothed or vested with a robe of authority and/or stands behind a pulpit upon which there is a Bible. Again the law/gospel distinction and the uses thereof are the pattern. The Bible is exposited in a historical-redemptive way with Jesus as the central character, since that is the way Jesus taught us to view the Scriptures (John 5:39; Luke 24:13–49).

There are the prayers of the people. In more liturgical settings the minister will turn around and face forward, leading the people in prayer, as they stand and corporately recite "hear our prayer" after each petition. Through Christ, we may boldly approach the Father. We need not constantly say, as is the common practice today in pop evangelicalism, "Father, we just" or "Father, I just" before our requests, as if we don't want to bother him too much.

A substantive congregational prayer is one of the important elements that many marketing movement churches have shed. It's simply not something that appeals to consumers, if that's what you're trying to do. As Pastor Kim Riddlebarger has pointed out, when consumerism becomes the focus and you are trying to attract people with a cool product, "who cares about Erma's goiter!? Someone who's a seeker is not going to care about Erma ... [or] about sin."[1] Many evangelical pastors, having abdicated their responsibility to provide congregational prayer in their services, then try to fill

1. Riddlebarger, "Worldiness."

the void that is created. Scolding their congregants for not being people of prayer, the weary are often guilt tripped into attending weeknight prayer meetings after having put in long days in their various vocations. What could be good, voluntary opportunities for more prayer is turned into yet another hoop to jump through.

There may be the recitation of one of the three historic creeds of the church (Apostles', Nicene, and Athanasian) setting forth the very basic facts of what it is that God's people believe. Though the churches vary in the frequency of the administration of the sacraments, there is also baptism and/or the Lord's Supper, visible signs and seals of God's gospel promises. These again are primarily means of grace, liberal and generous gifts from God, not primarily our means of commitment to God which is the popular contemporary notion. Baptism is concerned with our initiation into new life and faith, being born of water and Spirit by the Word for the forgiveness of sins. Communion or the Lord's Supper is a participation or communion with the body and blood of Christ. It is a further visible and tangible nourishment of our union with Christ, employing all of our senses: sight, touch, taste, smell and hearing. Again we see the uses of the law and the gospel at work.

Speaking of which, the service then concludes not with a mere dismissal, but with a *bene* ("good") *diction* ("word") or parting blessing, as it is sometimes called. This follows the biblical pattern which we find both in the Old Testament (Aaronic blessing) as well as at the end of the various New Testament letters (epistles) intended to be read as sermons in the early church. What is the Lord's good word that he leaves with his people? Peace. Through Jesus our mediator whose work is applied by the Holy Spirit, we have peace with God the Father and are yet again reminded of that as we begin a new week of service to our neighbor out of gratitude to God.

The church desperately needs to return to at least the basic biblical elements of worship, and, in many cases, the biblical theology which under girds them. One or two generations of people bored with liturgy, who, instead of returning to the rich meaning of these elements, subsequently became innovators and left the church service decimated of its rich biblical content and meaning. We have, for all intents and purposes, turned it into a circus. *It has become all about the greatest show on earth instead of the greatest story ever told.*

This is not meant to suggest that all evangelical churches ought to simply rigidly adopt an old Anglican or Lutheran liturgy with their accompanying formality and ritual. To do so in contemporary popular culture would require something akin to an art history or art appreciation course that colleges offer. Not that this would necessarily be a bad idea in many cases, but it is the essence, the substantive elements of worship that are key, not merely the form. Certainly the form can be more contemporary. For example, the *Kyrie* works very well with acoustic guitars (not to mention that for many millennials, their only exposure to pipe organ music is from watching scary movies). For some, it may involve a long and gradual process to restore the basic biblical elements of worship. It can involve the simplest of improvements. While out of town, I had occasion to visit a Baptist church with a very scant liturgy. Yet the offertory celebrated God's gifts to us and who we are in him with a simple chorus based on 1 John 3:1: "See what kind of love the Father has given to us, that we should be called children of God." The service wasn't perfect, but that little gem was enough to remind the people that it was about receiving his gifts. Another time, while visiting an Anglican church which was otherwise pretty dreary and tired with a sermon empty of gospel joy, the more elaborate liturgy ensured gospel proclamation. It included a comforting reminder from the beautiful hymn "Glorious Things of Thee Are Spoken" that Jesus is the never-ending fountain of living water and in him we will never be left to thirst. The people sang that old classic verse "Who can faint while such a river, ever flows their thirst ta' sauge!"[2] (meaning to quench). Again, the service was far from ideal, but because God's gifts were conveyed and received in faith, it was enough. The thirsting were assuaged and through this refreshing time of Sabbath rest, the congregants had the wind at their backs once again for a new week.

Finally, many pop evangelicals have reported having bad experiences growing up in Roman Catholicism, thereby often creating an aversion to all things liturgical. It is very important for these evangelicals to remember that the Roman Catholic and Greek Orthodox churches also come out of the same early church history and tradition that Protestant evangelicals do. Whatever distortions of the truth that existed and/or may exist in them, which the Reformers sought to, and still seek to correct, never meant they were totally devoid of the truth. Therefore, there are plenty of things that may sound Roman Catholic or with which one may associate a bad experience with liturgy which, upon closer examination, we find are thoroughly biblical in and of themselves. For example, following a historic liturgy and

---

2. John Newton, "Glorious Things of Thee Are Spoken," in *Psalter Hymnal*, no. 402.

singing the *Agnus Dei* (Latin for "Lamb of God") before communion is simply to recite John 1:29. Similarly, singing the *Nunc Dimittis* (Latin for "Now You Dismiss") following communion is simply to recite the Song of Simeon in Luke 2.

It is interesting that well-known Anglican author and ESV Study Bible editor J. I. Packer acknowledges that when he was young, the Anglican Book of Common Prayer liturgy "bored me stiff." He goes on to say:

> Over the years [I have] found the historic Anglican Prayer Book to be a source of increasing delight and excitement (I choose my words; I mean them) so that now in my eighth decade I find myself valuing it more than at any earlier time in my life ... I came to see that the root problem with the Prayer Book (if "problem" is the right word) is not that its language is ceremonial in an old-fashioned way, but that it is a spiritual book for spiritually alive people, and you cannot expect anyone to be other than bored with it until Jesus Christ renews their hearts and the Bible itself begins to open up to them. So, now in my eighth decade, I am more of an enthusiast for the Prayer Book than ever. I am increasingly grateful for what it gives me. I find that during the past ten years I have spoken and written more on its behalf than ever before.[3]

He writes that services should instruct and edify: "The quest today is for services that will express what people have in their hearts at the moment, rather than put into their hearts what they need to grasp if they are ever to grow in grace and please God—that is one reason why today's alternative service forms are so shallow and flat."[4] He says that we urgently need to recover the true wisdom of training up the people, rather than watering down the faith. Even Billy Graham has remarked that if he had it to do over again, he would do so as an Evangelical Anglican as he saw spiritual beauty in Anglican order.[5]

The bottom line is that people are sinners. Our sin is what messes up both organized formal liturgy and more freewheeling spontaneity. The former can end up in a rote mindless ritual, the latter can end up in a circus. The current state of affairs in pop evangelicalism would suggest we are suffering more from the circus atmosphere and that we need to recover some order and formality. At least a basic liturgy, even with utilizing

---

3. Packer, "Rooted and Built Up in Christ."
4. Ibid.
5. Cole, "Billy Graham."

contemporary musical instruments, would tend to better preserve the basic elements of worship that we find in the Bible.

8

Keeping Time with Two Calendars

MANY OLD REFORMATION CHURCHES did (and still do in some cases) services at the beginning and end of every Lord's Day, and other times like Ascension Day. Understanding that those may have been simpler times, the people of the past arguably had less distraction and more time. Without becoming legalistic on either side of this issue, weekly morning and evening services are probably not a realistic option for many churches. We would do well, however, to at least reorientate ourselves to the fact that we are citizens of two kingdoms and have two different calendars.

Most evangelical churches today, both pop and Reformational, have long forgotten their Christian calendar and how it bears witness to this present passing age of our citizenship in the age to come. Obsessed with this passing age, *our weekly church celebrations now revolve more around Hallmark greeting card days than the days of God's mighty acts* (Ps 145). The great milestone days of celebration in the church have become Super Bowl Sunday, Mother's Day, Memorial Day, Father's Day, graduation, and Fourth of July and even the secular version of Halloween, which ironically was once a holiday of the church, All Hallow's Eve (which coincidentally is Reformation Day, as well). While Christmas and Easter still make the list, as well, most would have no idea when Ascension Day even is, much less its tremendous significance. It is the culmination of Jesus' completion of his mission on earth, triumphantly returning to the Father in glory to present his finished work so that the benefits could begin to be delivered on Pentecost through the Holy Spirit. Today the weekly Lord's Day has lost its status as a holy day as well. This day was graciously set apart by God for his people to rest from their good and common activities and to participate in the powers of the age to come as the kingdom of God breaks in on the present evil age through the proclaiming of the forgiveness of sins.

It wasn't always this way. Continuing the liturgical tradition of the early church, English reformer Thomas Cranmer in the seventeenth century produced the Anglican liturgical Book of Common Prayer (BCP) referred to above. Subsequently other denominations developed their own derivatives of the BCP. Many churches of the Reformation specifically followed, and many still do follow, the BCP's church year or lectionary as it is called. The one year or three year lectionary of Scripture readings would serve as the menu for the weekly diet in the liturgy. The Reformational church understood that its weekly celebrations were defined by a different calendar of events. The church year began with Advent, followed by the twelve days of Christmastide, followed by the season of Epiphany, Lent, Good Friday, Easter, Ascension Day, Pentecost and the Season of the Church. The weekly service was shaped by the world of the Bible, not this world. Similarly, other Reformational churches, such as the Reformed, did not as strictly use the church year lectionary as its guide, but were guided by the fifty two Lord's Day celebrations set forth in the Heidelberg catechism. Either way, the intent was that the flock would be protected by ensuring that the pastor covered the major Christian teachings of redemption each year. In both cases the emphasis was on shaping the service according to the great events of God in redemptive history and not by the trite holidays of this passing age. Certainly secular holidays can and do provide the church occasion to remember fathers, mothers, veterans and others in various ways; however, these days never ought to redefine the Lord's Day or his service.

9

The Bar Stool

WHATEVER DIFFERENCES THE REFORMATION churches had in their architecture and layout, they all had in common three basic pieces of furniture: the pulpit, the altar or the Lord's (communion) table and the baptismal font. The Worship or Divine Service was God's primarily appointed place where he promised to dispense his gifts of grace through the preaching of the Word (law and gospel) and the administration of the sacraments (baptism and the Lord's supper). Thus, these three pieces of furniture signified and served these three primary elements of worship. The layout may have varied. Presbyterians, Reformed, Baptists and Congregationalists, partly modeling their churches after the synagogue, had the pulpit in the center to emphasize the primacy of the preaching of the Word. Anglicans and Lutherans, on the other hand, partly modeling their churches after the temple, had the altar in the center emphasizing Christ's presence. The baptismal font was also prominently displayed in all Reformational traditions. As we have observed, both sacraments were viewed primarily as his means of grace, i.e., the promise of the gospel made visible, not primarily as our means of commitment. It was understood that we don't baptize ourselves, but rather that we are baptized; that we don't feed ourselves in communion, but rather that we are fed.

It was in this context that the minister, God's appointed servant, would fulfill his functions of Word and Sacrament ministry. As we have also seen, his office would be manifest not only by the pulpit behind which he stood, but also by a clerical vestment of some sort, signifying his office. Again,

The Bar Stool

there were variations, ranging from a suit similar to what a lawyer would wear as an officer of the court, to more extravagant robes similar to what a judge would wear to signify his office, to just a cross hanging around his neck. His job was simply to break open the word of God and deliver God's good gifts to the people. The three pieces of furniture were all there to serve this function.

With revivalism, the centrality and use of this furniture began to erode. Then over the course of just three short decades or so, from about 1970 to 2000, this furniture completely disappeared from many churches, giving way first to the Plexiglas lectern and then came the bar stool. Cool, casual, and conversational, this is the piece of furniture usually at the center of today's worship along with a drum set, guitars, amplifiers, cords and music stands all laid out on a stage or "platform" as some more diplomatically refer to it. This is where many pastors now deliver the "message" when they are not "roaming the stage." The church marketers have completely redesigned the worship area in only one generation.

Concededly, the issue is not about the furniture *per se*. In fact, there is nothing wrong with a pulpit made of Plexiglas and a case could be made for bringing God's word from a sitting position. An elevated pulpit, though, compared with horizontal, relational furniture, suggests an elevated Word. Ultimately, the underlying issue for worship concerns "the internal posture before God."[1] Sadly this change in furniture often does, in fact, reveal a much more significant and ominous shift. The place for God's appointed means of grace is often turned into an entertainment venue.

No longer dispensing God's good gifts by heralding the good news, Pastor Hip is now doing the Oprah Winfrey show or Dr. Phil or Comedy Central. He's funny, hip, emotional, ostensibly authentic and transparent, helpful and practical. He's light, but he's all advice (law) with little or no gospel. He leaves the people tickled, but increasingly malnourished. The spotlight has shifted from Christ in his saving office to Pastor Bob and his practical tips for living. In short, he's not offering anything different than the culture, and Oprah, Dr. Phil, and Comedy Central do that a lot better.

---

1. Wells, "Courage to Be Protestant."

10

The Mystical, Gnostic, Sentimental Christian (the One Standing out in the Meadow with Raised Arms)

The churches of the Reformation also have always varied somewhat on their views of images in the worship sanctuary due to differing interpretations of the Ten Commandments. For the Orthodox Presbyterians it would be a dangerous risk of idolatry to even have a plain cross in the worship area. The churches of other denominations might have a cross along with simple stained glass windows. On the other end of the spectrum, the Anglicans and Lutherans would have stained glass images of Christ and other biblical figures. Be that as it may, none of them portrayed the new symbolism now often portrayed in the contemporary church.

Upon entering a contemporary worship service, the dominant image one is confronted with is a solitary, semi-hippie looking woman or man standing in a meadow, or by the ocean, or on a mountain, with arms outstretched to the heavens. This modern image, projected on screens throughout evangelical churches, has all but replaced the cross as the major symbol of Christianity. Just tune to your cable television's contemporary Christian music channel and there she (or he) will be.

The gnostic impulse inside all of us is very strong. In a broad way it is associated with many and varied names: gnostics, mystics, enthusiasts, transcendentalists, romantics, sentimentalists, pagans and hippies are but a few. (We could also add some names associated with Christianity:

The Mystical, Gnostic, Sentimental Christian

monastic monks, pietists and those seeking the "Higher Life.") The general idea of Gnosticism is that by the shedding of institutions, society, people and the physical realm, I can, through a secret knowledge derived in my inner, emotional mystical experience, ever ascend closer to the presence of God. The problem, of course, is that no one is capable of building such a ladder. While we're trying in private solitude to climb up the ladder of mystical experience to God, God in his grace and mercy is climbing down and meeting us, not in solitude, but as a publicly assembled people, in the physical realm. He does so through his Son taking on the flesh of humanity and continues to do so through the institution of the church with ordinary means such as words, bread, wine and water. *If meditating upward by yourself in a meadow or on a mountain or by the ocean to "connect" with God is where it's really at, your children have got to wonder—why are we coming to church at all?!* Yes, God is generally present everywhere such as in nature, but it is where the Word is proclaimed and sacraments administered that he promises to be present in his saving work.

Sure, we can and should pray out in nature. Sure, we have the freedom to raise our arms in praise and thanksgiving. Sure, we can do yoga-like stretches. The problem is that we have too often synchronized the Christian faith with the Age of Aquarius. We often hear the charge of synchronization from evangelicals who point out that Christianity is often fused with paganism in places like South America. What American evangelicals do not realize is that we are often guilty of the very same thing. Many Christians have deluded themselves into thinking that the god they are seeking is not the pagan god within, but God himself. In fact, it is often an idol of our own making that we seek rather than the One revealed to us outside of ourselves in Word and Sacrament. The Woodstock generation has greatly fueled our propensity for self-salvation by mystical ascent. Instead we need to be hearers and receivers of him who "descends to us"[1] in our weakness to deliver us. He is no more near as when the gospel is preached (Rom 10). Martin Luther learned the hard way. After impeccably living the monastic life attempting to shed his worldliness and ascend ever closer to God, he found that even as he sat in the monk's cell, "I still had that rascal [his sinful human nature] right there with me."

Another species of the pagan genre, beside Gnosticism and mysticism, that has worked its influence into contemporary Christianity is sentimentalism. While stoicism consists in not allowing any emotion,

---

1. Calvin, *Commentaries*, Psalm 42:1–3.

sentimentalism consists in only allowing the positive emotions. The end result is that often what feels good or what is popular will substitute for clarity of biblical thinking. Biblical thinking, being thoroughly realistic, deals with the good and the bad, the positives and the negatives. It's ultimately about the truth, positive or negative, not about being positive at any cost. While we are not to judge anyone's standing before God, Christians are instructed to judge between right and wrong, truth and falsehood, the biblical and the unbiblical. Thus, when it comes to our responses to the wrong, the false, and the unbiblical, there ought to be an appropriate measure of negativity in addition to offering up the positive alternatives! The Bible teaches that the truth will set you free, not positive emotions or positive speech or faith in faith.

Two popular preachers from the 1960s and '70s were very influential in bringing this way of thinking into the Christian church: Norman Vincent Peale, with his emphasis on the power of positive thinking and Robert Schuller, with his television program, "Hour of Power." Also, vast segments of Pentecostal Christianity, in particular, have been heavily influenced by such secular thinking. The word-faith movement mistakenly views faith as a muscle which must be exercised in a positive way through positive speech. Only positive emotions and speech are to be allowed. Negative emotions and speech are seen as the enemy and are to be suppressed. Much of the contemporary Christian music industry, as well, is heavily influenced by this Christianized version of sentimentalism. The tagline for one Christian radio network is "the positive, encouraging sound." Much of contemporary Christian music itself can be classified simply as semi-paganism with a Christian label slapped on top.

This is further related to the resulting phenomenon of people then putting their faith in faith, rather than the object of their faith. As a result, many evangelicals are constantly struggling with and are anxious about the quality of their faith. Michael Horton relates the story of a pastor confiding to another pastor the doubts he was feeling and the daunting prospect as to whether or not his weak faith would carry him across the great chasm between here and heaven as he approached his death. The other pastor rightly reminded him to examine the steel girders of the sturdy bridge that spanned the chasm and to take his eyes off of himself. He was basically saying to keep our eyes fixed on Jesus, the object of our faith, rather than faith itself. It really mattered little whether he would walk boldly or with tentative apprehension. It was the bridge that was strong to save.

11

Forgiveness Is Good for the Soul

HAVING BEEN CALLED AND welcomed by the Most High in a Reformational Divine Service, the people come face to face with the reality of his holiness and righteousness and their lack of righteousness and holiness through the reading of his law. Lutherans, rather than reading the law in the service, recommend the reading of the Ten Commandments prior to the service to prepare for confession and absolution. Following the biblical pattern that we find, for example in Isaiah 6, the people then confess their sins and sinful state together in words or sometimes by singing a Psalm or hymn such as "God Be Merciful to Me" or "Lord, Like the Publican I Stand." Reformational theology properly recognizes that sin is not merely an act or an omission, but is a condition with which we are afflicted. First and foremost, we are not sinners because we sin; rather, we sin because we are sinners. Moreover, Christians continue to be simultaneously justified (saint) and sinner throughout their entire lives on this earth.

Having confessed their sinfulness, they are driven to Christ and all his benefits. This was supposed to be the uses of the law and gospel at work in the heart of the weekly service. The pastor then announces the forgiveness of sins in Christ. For the Reformed, it was called a declaration or assurance of pardon, for contemporary Presbyterians, the time of renewal, for the Lutherans, a declaration of absolution. Yes, Christians are forgiven of all their sins, past, present and future when they are justified, i.e., when they become Christians. For those who think there's never a need to hear forgiveness again, Pastor Jeremy Rhode wisely reminds us that *this would*

Part 2: How We Do Church

be like a husband saying he never needs to say "I love you" because he already said it once upon a time on his wedding day![1] With respect to man's side, i.e., his perpetual confession of sin and turning to Christ, G. I. Williamson puts it this way: "[Repentance and faith] are divine gifts (Acts 11:18, Eph 2:8). When God regenerates the soul, he implants the seed (or beginning) of repentance and faith. It is improper therefore to think of either repentance or faith as mere momentary acts of the soul, they are rather permanent states or conditions expressive of the soul. We may speak of the initial act of repentance and faith. But with this initial act begins an activity that never ceases thereafter (Luke 22:32)."[2] Many biblical examples could be cited of this: David ("my sin is ever before me"); Isaiah ("I am a man of unclean lips"); and, Paul ("I am [not was] the chief of sinners"). The Lord himself taught us this pattern when he taught us how we ought to pray together ("forgive us our trespasses").

Over the years this process could get watered down and many Reformational churches didn't quite get it completely right. Maybe they got intimidated by the attempted improvements to Scripture, i.e., the do-it-yourself-ism that John Wesley and Charles Finney propagated and which became so popular in America, that they started to hold back on grace. Whatever the case, the accent always seemed to fall on the law and the guilt. Always talking about the cancer without the miraculous cure would later cause many to go into denial and opt for happy clappy worship.

It took me many years before I understood, that this process of going back to the law and the gospel was designed by God for me to consciously run to Christ and hide in him, united to him and covered by him. I needed to be constantly reminded of his perfect passive obedience on the cross imputed to me for the forgiveness of my sins and his perfect, lifelong, active obedience imputed to me so that I know that my judgment has already been rendered—a gracious definitively assured declaration to me in Christ of "well done, good and faithful servant!" *He justifies me just as if I've never sinned and just as if I've always obeyed.* The law could then be my friend and Mt. Sinai would no longer thunder at me. Despite all my imperfections and failures, the law could never accuse me. "There is therefore now no condemnation for those who are in Christ Jesus" (Rom 8:1). Would I now live a life just taking advantage and licentiously abusing such a ridiculously generous arrangement? No, there was more to this gospel, a promise

---

1. See Rhode, "Gospel for Former [Pop] Evangelicals."
2. Williamson, *Westminster Confession*, 98–99.

that he would work in me so that I can begin to walk in newness of life, guided by the law as a rule of gratitude and that the work he began in me will be brought to completion (Rom 6; Col 2:13; Phil 1:6). Wow! I finally understood the Scriptures. It was this biblical clarity recovered during the Protestant Reformation, which came to be known as Reformation theology, that, among other things, turned the world upside down. It was what inspired so many great accomplishments, including such musical classics as: Calvinist John Newton's "Amazing Grace," Calvinist Augustus Toplady's "Rock of Ages, Cleft for Me," Lutheran Bach's "Jesu, Joy of Man's Desiring," and Lutheran Handel's "Messiah."

When churches began to distort this wonderful gospel orientated practice into a law orientated practice, instead of a time of great comfort and joy, it became an uncomfortable moment in the service. Then it wasn't long before it got abbreviated to confession without any mention of forgiveness at all and, then, eventually disposed of altogether. Most pop evangelical churches never had this practice in the first place due to their limited view of sin as merely consisting of certain outward acts. They failed to see the serious condition of sin as ongoing in the life of the Christian. This influence only facilitated the demise of this practice in many Reformational churches. Perhaps confession also just didn't feel appropriate for a culture overly saturated with "I Am Special," which eventually blossomed into the selfie culture.

Instead of the gospel both igniting and fueling the Christian life, Christians have fallen into the trap warned of by the Apostle Paul: "Having begun by the Spirit, are you now being perfected by the flesh?" (Gal 3:3). To gut this weekly loving reminder of forgiveness from the weekly service is to gut it from the life of the Christian. To merely tell congregants to clean up their act and straighten themselves out denies us two important weekly gifts we need. We need to be reminded both of the cleansing bath we are given for the forgiveness of sins and our being reclothed with the righteousness of Christ that he lovingly provides for our encouragement.

12

The Church Was Not Born Yesterday

When Reformational churches began to lose their rich liturgical identity, usually one of the first things that went, beside the time of confession and forgiveness was the reciting of the Apostles' or Nicene Creed. The church was instituted by Christ himself some two thousand years ago. He used twelve men known as the apostles to establish this worldwide institution. They laid the foundational teachings and the Word spread through preaching, teaching, baptism and the Lord's Supper. Churches were established, local elders were appointed to oversee them and pastors were ordained to shepherd them. Thus the baton passed from these twelve specially chosen ones whose authority was manifest by extraordinary signs and wonders to succeeding generations of ordinary ministers. The creeds of the church set forth the foundational teachings of the apostles.

The Roman Catholic Church claims to be the true apostolic church because of its succession of authoritative magisterial bishops following Peter. The Eastern Orthodox Church claims to be the true apostolic church because it traces its roots to the churches at Jerusalem and Antioch, established before the church was established in Rome. A lot of pop evangelicals, particularly Pentecostals, claim to be the true apostolic church with their many local apostles, the "anointed ones," claiming magisterial authority in multiple local congregations. This is even expanding by the recent trend of churches having multi-sites, something foreign to the Bible. If not outright popery, these churches' pastors have become the new self-appointed archbishops of American pop evangelicalism.

The Church Was Not Born Yesterday

The Reformers taught that the true apostolic church is where the foundational teachings of the apostles are most faithfully and accurately carried forward to succeeding generations. The church stands under the authority of the Word, not above it. The church's authority is ministerial, not magisterial. This understanding of the church as institutionally apostolic has been lost. Because pop evangelicals are so thin on history, there is this huge gap between the apostles of the New Testament and nineteen hundred years later when Billy Sunday comes along. Many are at a loss to explain the historical connections and as a result of this (and failing to properly distinguish between law and gospel), many pop evangelicals jump ship to the Roman church or the Eastern Church.

The church has been around for a while. Being a member of the church necessarily constitutes membership in an institution that has endured through numerous generations for over two thousand years. For the American pop evangelical, the church fathers are Rick Warren, maybe Billy Graham and, perhaps for the more historically-minded, Billy Sunday. It is a travesty that the pop churches have so cut themselves off from the past. Not only has the apostolic connection been lost, but so has any appreciation for the church fathers—those of our leaders in the early history of the church. The wisdom accumulated throughout the ages on issues that every generation deals with has largely been lost. Names such as Polycarp, Irenaeus, Augustine, Bernard of Clairvaux, are utterly meaningless to pop evangelicals.

Not only the fathers, but the confessions of the Protestant churches have all but been lost on this generation. The ecumenical creeds of the church had set forth the basic facts of the faith. From early church history on, Christians would recite what they believe as set forth in the Apostles' Creed, the Nicene Creed, and the Athanasian Creed during the Divine Service. During the Reformation and following, it became apparent to the Reformers that summaries of other essential biblical teachings should be formulated as well. For instance, you could affirm the facts of the Apostles' Creed and still get the teachings of Scripture mixed up on important topics such as justification and sanctification. Therefore, the main streams of the Reformation formulated summaries of what they felt were the essential teachings of Scripture. These were set forth in their confessions and companion question and answer teaching tools known as catechisms. A section from the Reformation confessions and catechisms would often be read or recited in the service in addition to the Apostles' or Nicene Creed. As stated above, what is remarkable are the similarities of the confessions. All of them were united on some basic essentials in what became to be known as the *solas* of the Reformation: *sola Scriptura* (Scripture alone); *solus Christus* (Christ alone); *sola Gratia* (Grace alone); *sola Fide* (Faith alone); and *sola Deo Gloria* (the Glory of God alone). That is, based upon the authority of Scripture alone, salvation is by grace alone through faith alone in Christ alone to the glory of God alone. It was the word "alone" in each instance which distinguished the churches of the Reformation from the Church of Rome.

What is so beneficial from having written confessions, is that we have the Spirit-guided wisdom of multiple generations from multiple countries and continents spelling out basic teachings of Scripture that have withstood the tests of time. They address the essential questions that every generation of thinking Christians have had to deal with. Without focusing on the differences of these confessions which came out of the Reformation, evangelicals would make a quantum leap forward if they were able to take just the areas of agreement and at least make that their confession. What evangelicals are doing now is living off of the skewed thoughts of a few people who rebelled and went their own way, but who were largely influential in the formation of American pop evangelicalism. *While they now usually attempt to identify themselves as generic Christian churches who just follow the Bible, the fact of the matter is that they are preaching a blend of Arminianism, Wesleyanism, Finneyism and Hybelism.* The Bible is a big book and there have been a multitude of interpretations of it. Thoughtful Christians must take responsibility for which ones are in fact most faithful to the text and consistent with the whole. Does anyone really believe that Billy Sunday, Charles Finney or Bill Hybels were right in their implicit, if not explicit, rejection of some basic understandings of multitudes of prior leaders such as Luther, Calvin, Charles Haddon Spurgeon, Jonathan Edwards, B. B. Warfield and the Westminster Divines? Do we really think that Beth Moore or Sarah Young has more to offer than the treasures of the past? We certainly act like it when it comes to what we emphasize. Like forgiveness, restoring some reading or recitation of the creeds and confessions in the service would also be good for the soul.

13

Music
The Great Exchange and the Need to Preserve Open Space

NOT BORN YESTERDAY—SO IT is with the music of the church as well. The church's musical repertoire has developed over the course of its own two thousand year history as well as its incipient existence for thousands of years before that in the nation of Israel. There are the OT Psalms. There are the songs of Zechariah, Mary, and Simeon and the doxologies of the NT. There are the early ancient hymns of the church fathers such as "Let All Mortal Flesh Keep Silence." The songs of the historical church are richly loaded with content. Part of Christians singing responsively to God together as a church was also the desire that the Word of God might dwell richly in each other (Col 3:16). Kim Riddlebarger has compared the collections of psalms and hymns in psalters and hymnals to a giant glacier where some chunks which can't carry the weight eventually fall away, while other songs get added on through succeeding generations.

The American pop evangelical church of the Boomer and X generations has had little understanding or appreciation of this. They regard their own generations as normative in setting the agenda and, in doing so, have become exclusionary. They have their pop music to allegedly substitute for that of the previous generation. What they don't realize is that the prior generations generally were not singing their pop music— the music of the

'40s and '50s, whether big band or country. They were singing the praises that had been passed on to them over multiple centuries and countless generations. There were ordinary and common genres of music for everyday and then there was the sacred music of the church service. Perhaps part of the problem is that there was a lot of pop stuff added to the hymnals of revivalist evangelicals beginning in the late nineteenth century which was a fusion of pop entertainment culture with the music of the church. This had coincided with the Romantic/Transcendental movements which was faddish in nature. This, in turn, gave way to new secular trends as time passed, such as Frank Sinatra–inspired special musical selections in pop evangelical services. These compromising influences only fueled the later wholesale replacement of hymnals with contemporary pop music by the church marketers. For the most part, songs used to be seriously vetted by many pastors and elders and certified as safe for the flock's consumption before making it into a good hymnal. Today this responsibility has largely been abdicated. Often one never knows what lyrics a teenage "worship leader" might have programmed to pop up on the big screen for consumption by the flock.

This is not to say that there should not be new songs or new instruments. Words in old hymns like "gladly for aye" are definitely outdated now and often need to be updated. And sure, there is room for other instruments and some contemporary arrangements. For instance, Indelible Grace and High Street Hymns are attempting to bring a fresh contemporary sound to some of the ancient hymns which are so rich in content. Too many traditionalists, trying to be holier than God, mistakenly view all guitars and percussion in worship as inherently evil—much like many fundamentalists would look at a glass of merlot (Ps 150; Ps 104:14–15).

While this is not to say that there should be no new songs or no new instruments, it is to say that the lyrics should be biblically sound and the music reverent and God-glorifying. It ought not to trivialize God or be all about me. It ought to avoid mystical repetition. It ought to be gospel driven, not market driven. Frankly, the congregation ought to at least be aware when a song is not in the public domain and when the church is paying for the right to sing it. It ought not to contribute to the juvenilization of the church, but should be carefully vetted with the wisdom of the elders.

Like the Psalms, it should be expressive of the range of human emotion, from lament to joyful praise. Pop evangelicals know very little laments and penitential songs. It is usually happy clappy pop choruses that are "poor imitations of the American Top 40"[1] pop chart songs that predominate. By nature we don't want to mourn our sin or hear the great wedding music about Christ to whom we are betrothed. We are always striving for a counterfeit Easter without Good Friday. As Jesus said to the Pharisees, "We played the flute for you, and you did not dance; we sang a dirge, and you did not mourn" (Matt 11:17). There ought to be a time to express our sorrow for sin and the putting to death of our sinful nature, even as we celebrate our coming alive in our union with Christ. Our propensities in music are similar to C. S. Lewis' famous remark that we tend to satisfy ourselves with making mud pies in the slum, when we could be enjoying a "holiday at the sea."[2] What is ironic is that many of the pop stars of secular music have a better understanding of the difference between the music of pop culture and music that can carry the weight of eternal truths. When mega pop star of the '60s and '70s Robin Gibbs of the Bee Gees died, his family and friends included the eighth-century hymn "Be Thou My Vision" at his funeral, which, by the way, includes the poignant line: "riches I heed not, nor man's empty praise."[3]

There is no doubt that future generations will look back with astonishment at the wholesale change in church music attempted to be made by evangelical church marketing boomers and their children. They will truly wonder: what were the boomers thinking, shutting down world class organs across the country and often exchanging them for something some consider to be "hillbilly" music?[4] As the pendulum swings, it is only a matter of time before large segments of evangelicalism will once again join the rest of the church in singing the magnificent, historic hymns of the church, such as Advent's "Lo! He Comes with Clouds Descending," Easter morning's "The Strife Is O'er, the Battle Done" or "Hallelujah, What a Savior!" and All Saints Day's "For All the Saints."

Furthermore, there is no question that we have, in fact, traded a lot more away than the organ for electric guitars. While there are appropriate

---

1. Horton, *Better Way*, 177.

2. Lewis, *Weight of Glory and Other Addresses*, 1–2.

3. "Be Thou My Vision," Irish, 8th c., translated by Mary E. Byrne, in *Trinity Hymnal*, no. 642.

4. See *Reformed Churchmen*, "Crown Him with Many Crowns."

ways to use both the organ and guitars in the service, in the wholesale trade of one for the other, we have clearly given up more than the organ and have received in return a lot of extra baggage with the guitars. The problem goes so much deeper than the music itself. It is, in fact, something beyond the music that is really the issue.

Why is it that no one seems to notice there's usually so much more going on than just an exchange of instruments? *It's rarely just the guitars replacing the organ. It's usually the guitars replacing the pulpit, Lord's Table and baptismal font.* In Reformational Christianity at its best, God is the main actor in the service and gets center stage. It is primarily about what he is doing through the mediated means of grace which he has ordained: the proclaiming of the Word and administering the sacraments of baptism and the Lord's Supper. Music has its secondary purpose in the people's responses to what God is doing through his servant, the minister. The people never sang song after song after song, usurping the lead role. That role belonged to God alone. The organ was never given center stage (nor was it applauded). It always pointed toward the front, even if sideways. It was never set front and center on a stage facing the congregation and replacing pulpit, table and font. There was in the front and center a sacred open space marked by this furniture and sometimes a cross.

In much of American pop evangelicalism, on the other hand, the people are the main actors in the service and the people take center stage while we imagine God sits in "passive appreciation"[5] (presumably tapping his foot to the beat). It is primarily about what the people are doing through their means of commitment that they have ordained: attempting to emotionally and mystically connect with God through extended praise choruses, celebrating our deeds and giving each other practical tips for living the life of good works. It is usually led by a man in jeans called Bob or Phil. He is not seen as someone who is God's servant, an ordained office bearer who should be addressed as Reverend or Pastor. He is not even vested with a suit jacket or standing behind a pulpit, but is simply viewed as one of us. It is a power plant theology where I am the plug. God is the socket as a resource for me and my life, into which I need to directly (immediately) "plug in" or "connect" apart from the mediated means of grace.

Music becomes primary in such a context in trying to conjure God's presence in a semi-pagan sort of way. In this regard, Psalm 22:3 has been doubly misconstrued. Pastor Zac Hicks makes a good case for the New

---

5. Horton, *Better Way*, 180.

International Version rendering of this verse: "Yet you are enthroned as the Holy One; you are the one Israel praises" (NIV).[6] Other translations opt for God being enthroned on, or sometimes inhabiting, the praises of Israel. Even if these were accurate, instead of recognizing that God has established this assembly by his initiative where he sits enthroned on the praises of his people and reading it as a statement of fact of God's self-revelation, we mistake it as our way of conjuring him like the pagans conjure the spirits. Evangelical pastors routinely try to get their congregants to praise the Lord with more intensity, supposedly to get the Spirit to move, because God inhabits our praise. The word "because" or "as" or "for" is erroneously added to Scripture which ends up conveying the false idea that we should earnestly sing "so that our God will" inhabit our praise. This idea was further propagated by Russ Taff's popular 1970s praise song entitled "Praise the Lord."

While this is not to say that these churches have instituted pagan worship, it is to say that they have been influenced by pagan ideas. Anyone accustomed to traditional worship visiting a contemporary pop evangelical service will, after numerous back to back songs, invariably feel the question arising within: "will I ever be able to sit down and listen to what God has to say?" Here there is often mantra-like repetition until the mystical vibe has been attained, evidenced by a multitude of closed eyes and outstretched arms reaching up to the heavens. The scene actually becomes a spectacle ripe for parody as seen, for instance, in the article "Hand Raising Worship—the 10 Styles."[7]

In light of this focus in pop evangelicalism, the band always gets center stage, replacing, or at least overshadowing, pulpit, table and font. And never is the band faced toward the front in a worship posture toward that sacred open space; it is always in a performance posture. The band itself and their instruments have usurped that sacred open space.

The worship wars, more often than not, are really about two completely different theologies of worship.[8] To be sure there are issues related to the music and the lyrics, but those issues are really secondary to the larger picture. One hundred fifty years ago, lawyer-turned-preacher Charles Finney decided that God's Word was not enough. According to Finney, we had to put man at the center to pull himself up by his own bootstraps. To

---

6. See Hicks, "Is 'God Inhabits the Praises of His People' Really Biblical?"
7. Acuff, "Hand Raising Worship."
8. See Wilken, "Behind the Music."

do this, he instituted "new measures" which included pop entertainment style music and various motivational techniques all designed to manipulate the emotions of the people. No longer relying on God's means of grace, he effectively declared war on Reformational Christianity and American pop evangelicalism came of age. According to Finney, it was at his tent revivals, not traditional church services, where it was really happening. This is the cheaply built and uniquely American foundation upon which many of the contemporary megachurches have been built.

What is sad for the church is that there are countless third-, fourth-, and fifth-generation descendants of German Lutherans, Dutch Reformed, Scottish Presbyterians, English Anglicans, and others who understandably sought to shed the "old country" identities of their grandparents and to just worship as Americans. In doing so, however, they have been swept and duped into an evangelicalism made in America, largely invented by nineteenth-century revivalists and more recently modernized by the twentieth-century church marketers. They have all too eagerly, and often unknowingly, traded away their rich Reformation theological and liturgical heritage for an immature, impoverished and polluted version of Christianity. To exacerbate the situation, we now have new generations being brought up to think that they are inherently special and therefore don't need the wisdom of the prior generations which have gone before. There are numerous megachurch "pastors" out there, having little or no formal seminary training. While leading thousands, many are making the types of mistakes that even tenth graders in the catechism classes of a prior generation would not have made. While the churches of the older generations certainly had their faults, this wholesale change that has taken place in America represents a clear step back in the history of Christ's church. More importantly, it puts the next generation at very serious risk of losing the basics altogether, even as much of it is further being exported around the world. *Biblical worship is neither party, nor motivational lecture, nor social service agency meeting, nor pagan ritual.* It is to be graciously addressed by the living God with the living and active Word of God, through which he dispenses his amazing gifts, to which we appropriately respond with singing (along with offerings and prayers).

Is this an indictment of generation X and Y evangelicals? To be sure, their narcissism has been played upon in a big way and everyone bears responsibility. In the end, though, it's a much greater indictment of me and my generation. Sadly, we boomers may well go down in church history as the weakest link in the passing on of the faith from generation to generation, for we were the link in Christ's church between a generation that still had much of it and the generation that has lost much of it. It is now up to the Y's (a.k.a., the millennials) and the Z's (a.k.a., the igeneration) to reclaim what their hippie grandparents and narcissistic parents have left them deprived of.

We need to first address this theological issue which is often the real issue behind the music. Let's move our bands a little to the side, or perhaps down by the organ or where the organ normally would be if there were one.[9] This is a meeting where God addresses his people and they respond to him. The band should not get in the way of that by being interjected in a distracting and dominating performance posture. This problem appears to be particularly acute in smaller settings. The band should assist and facilitate this two-way meeting between God and his people. We need to stop amplifying the voices of a few over and above the congregation. By removing the performance element, we can restore the proper accompaniment function of a band or ensemble. Keeping the pulpit and/or table front and center throughout the service is an important symbolic reminder of what and who is supposed to be the focus of this meeting. Let's also stop pandering to unguided juvenile led worship and provide some wisdom to young musicians. Let's choose a healthy repertoire of songs from the church's catalogue, a catalogue that extends back not just decades or centuries, but over millennium. Let's remove ourselves from the ladders of mystical ascent and works righteousness and redirect the weekly spotlight back on Christ in his saving office where he descends to us in Word and Sacrament. We need to return the lead part in the drama of the church service back to him and *restore the biblical elements of worship for the distribution of his gifts, for it is our union with him that is the very lifeblood of the body.*

---

9. See Smith, "Open Letter to Praise Bands."

14

Newsflash
The Bible Is Not about You

We now turn, for the next few sections, to the preaching of the Word—the sermon. One of the primary ways the church service has tended to become human-centered is the way the Bible is read or interpreted as it is preached. This type of preaching (not to mention the plethora of the same type of books at the Christian bookstore) then feeds the way parishioners read the Bible in their personal devotions as well. Jesus, in addressing the Pharisees (John 5:39), and on the road to Emmaus (Luke 24:13–49), made it very clear what the Bible is all about from start to finish—himself.

Our propensity again is to get it all backwards. We want to make it all about us. We do this in at least two ways. Instead of reading the Bible the way that Jesus taught as a historical-redemptive narrative with Christ at the center, we turn the Bible into either a collection of moralisms or doctrines. When we read about Old Testament characters, for example, our tendency is to substitute ourselves for the character and find some universal moral lesson that we can apply to our lives. Entire books have been written consisting of Old Testament character studies with little or no attention given to why the story is there in the first place, i.e., its historical redemptive significance as it relates to Christ. One example is David. The lesson is usually that we all need to be like David and slay the different giants that we face in our lives. The fact that David was a murderer and an adulterer must then be ignored or relegated to an inconvenient footnote. The problem here is that there are many giants which we face in our lives that we will never be able to slay. As a matter of fact, Christians are pretty much promised persecution, even to the point of being killed, as were the apostles. Consequently, this type of positive thinking can lead to an endless cycle of despair. *David, in fact, is a type of Christ, not a type of me!* Christ is the one who would slay the giants of sin and death and save the whole nation. The cowering Israelite who needs a Savior to slay these giants is what I am! Ironically, this results in a much greater practical application for us. Like the Israelites chasing the Philistines far and wide as a result of David's work, this realization of Christ's ultimate work is what will trigger spontaneous and confident works of gratitude in us.

Even more than a type of Christ, David is part of the lineage of the coming promised one. He is part of the unfolding of the plan of redemption in history. Even the events in his life providentially point us to Christ. Even other characters in his story point us to Christ and our need for a Savior, such as Bathsheba's husband, Uriah, whose death consequently covered her sin. Had it not been for the innocent death of another, her husband in this case, she would have been stoned to death for her sin!

Just as dangerously, American pop evangelical pastors and conference speakers have notoriously held themselves out as transformed examples for the flock to emulate (until the most vociferous of them are usually arrested for something). Instead of under-shepherds pointing to the Great Shepherd, they point to themselves as the CEO. Everyone in the corporate business model of the church is expected to get busy and excel from one managerial level to the next. Soon being a busy high energy person starts getting equated with being more spiritual. People want to attain to being like that man or woman leader, usually good looking, confident and high energy. The problem is that this is one type of personality that most people don't have. This again leads to despair and is a far cry from the Apostle Paul's call to spirituality by being diligent and working quietly with your hands. John the Baptist demonstrated both true leadership and proper focus when he said, "He must increase, but I must decrease" (John 3:30).

Another way we distort the intent of God's word is to make it just about doctrine. We want to make it merely about our learning and acquiring more knowledge. The sacramental aspect is then lost and the preaching becomes merely pedagogical. The drama of God's actual saving presence becomes lost. Creating a void for drama, we will consequently want to create our own drama. History has shown that Pentecostal tendencies are often then inflamed in such a context. This is also similar to and related to the problem of repressing all expressions of joy in worship and the backlash it produces among many raised in such environments.

The preaching and the reading of God's Word is not primarily about your life or your acquisition of knowledge, but it is for you. It is real. It is true. It is alive with the power of God unto salvation and is accomplishing its purposes. It is the greatest story ever told.

15

The Message or the Massage

SIN AND DEATH ARE not the problems which people naturally want to concern themselves with. We would much rather suppress these and talk about our activity and surface level felt needs. Therefore, pop evangelicalism's attempts to get serious often results in doing a version of a television talk show or some other form of therapy to deal with things like our mistakes and lack of fulfillment. When churches dispose of God's law, confession of sin, and assurance of forgiveness, they have to replace it with something. That something usually means coming up with our own law and calling it the gospel! This happened both in the older fundamentalism with its heavy legalism as well as in contemporary pop evangelicalism with its "lite" version of legalism.

The thinking goes something like this. We all know Jesus died on the cross, so let's get to the important, relevant stuff. Every week we should talk about what we need to do. We realize that some of the older American pop evangelical fundamentalist churches which shared this view made ridiculous lists when they substituted for the Ten Commandments and then tried to make that the good news: no movies, no card playing, no alcohol, no skirts above the knee, and no dancing. We're more enlightened than that. Instead, let's talk about our doing community, our doing small groups, our doing "mission" (humanitarian) trips, our doing worship, our having a worship experience, our personal transformation, our transforming the culture, our being the gospel, our living the gospel, our doing social justice, our meeting felt needs and tastes—in a word, let's just preach ourselves and how wonderful our doing is. While "our doing" now has a different focus, the problem is that the focus is still all about our doing.

Now, there are many wonderful and noble things to do on the contemporary list, *but will the children of these churches know that even Mother Theresa needs a Savior?* Will they understand that our most righteous deeds are as filthy rags in the light of his incomprehensible Holiness and are only acceptable through the mediating work of Jesus? Will they understand that Cain brought his best and was still rejected? Will they understand why? Will they understand that God requires absolute perfection (Matt 5:48) a righteousness that exceeds that of the Pharisees? (Matt 5:20) Or will they, like the Pharisees, be deluded into thinking they are pulling it off? Or will they burn out, despair and walk away, knowing they can't pull it off? Or, if not that desperate, will the church languish in mediocrity, never maturing in the fullness of the knowledge and grace of Jesus Christ, never seeing the incredibly rich theological alpine vistas (2 Pet 3:18; Eph 3:18–19; Rom 11:33)?

Or, will they know that what God demands in his law, he graciously gives in the gospel? Will they know that who he is, what he has done and what he is doing is far more important than anything we can ever be or do? Will they know that the gospel is the important, relevant stuff, not just for unbelievers, but that it is the fertile soil for the growth of believers, the power of salvation which is both justification and sanctification? Will they know that the gospel is not something we can be or live, but is an announcement of good news that powerfully and miraculously creates the world of which it speaks, which we can then live in light of? In short, will the faith, once and for all entrusted to the saints, be passed on to the next generation (Deut 6:6–9); or, will this generation, like so many times in the history of God's people, neither know the Lord nor the work he had done for Israel? (Judg 2:10) Trying to overcome seemingly boring, dead orthodoxy with relevant therapy and deeds instead of dramatic life-giving preaching ultimately leads to death. It is to treat the peoples' serious wounds with Band-Aids (Jer 6:14; 8:11). It is to leave them malnourished with a fast-food diet (cf. John 21:15–17; Isa 55:1–2). This problem is further exacerbated by our technological age which is increasingly shortening the attention spans of succeeding generations. Minds are becoming even more averse to processing and digesting these important questions.

In the preaching of God's Word, there are two ancient heresies against which we must be ever vigilant. Both Pelagianism (do-it-yourself salvation by works, moralism, legalism) and Gnosticism (the religion of the inner self) arise naturally out of our sinful human nature. They are the natural default setting of every human heart. From the very beginning, they have always been welling up in the church and periodically needed to be warded off. We can see these basic conflicts in: Jesus vs. the Pharisees; the apostles vs. the Judaizers; Irenaeus vs. the early gnostics in the first century; Augustine vs. Pelagius in the fourth century, etc. By the early sixteenth century, these influences had gone unchecked for some time and, consequently, the teachings of medieval church became obscured by them. The Reformation then arose to restore the clarity of the gospel and the proper uses of the law and the gospel that had been present in the early church. These teachings were memorialized in the various written confessions and catechisms of the Reformation.

Regrettably, American pop evangelicalism, particularly beginning with Charles Finney and the other revivalists, and continuing through various Pietistic movements, brought these legalistic and gnostic influences back in a big way, again resulting in obscuring the clarity of the gospel. Legalism not only took the form of works righteousness, but also was comprised of adding laws where the Bible was silent. These influences ultimately created the heavy legalism of the twentieth-century fundamentalists (which, in turn, also heavily influenced Reformational churches), against which we now see a rebellion. The problem is that the rebellion against the legalism of the latter half of the twentieth century on into the twenty-first century has been misplaced. *Going from a heavy legalism to legalism "lite" is still legalism.* It is in the Reformation confessions and catechisms that the clear teachings of Scripture on these points is clearly laid out.

What is so very painfully tragic is that, not only have the descendants of fundamentalists fled to the law lite/ therapeutic concoction of the contemporary church marketing movement (or, worse yet, left the church completely), but so have the children of ostensibly Reformational churches who were fed heavy doses of legalism in the name of the Reformation. Unknown to them is that the legalism and mysticism which perpetually arise in the human heart didn't get fueled from true Reformational teaching, but rather was fueled by the influence of fundamentalist and pietistic teaching that had infused many Reformational churches. It is precisely the exposition of Scripture set forth in the Reformational confessions and catechisms that is what actually liberates us from this bondage. Many have sadly jumped from the frying pan into the fire. Legalistic, as well as mystical teachings, are, more often than not, actually fed, watered and memorialized in the Arminian/Wesleyan/Finneyan/Hybelian curriculum of pop evangelical churches, thereby trapping the unwary. Though it's now a lighter version and at first blush, a more smiley legalism, it is still bondage. It is still legalism and it is ultimately a silent killer that continues to leave many casualties in its wake.

One might be tempted to despair that so many have fled to churches that don't have a Reformational catechism or confession that actually contains the antidote to legalism and mysticism in their very precise and nuanced expositions of Scripture. It may look very bleak indeed when the curriculum of many pop churches only fuels these errors. It is here that we must go back to the source, Scripture itself, that living and active word and then rework the bad curriculums. A twenty-first-century reformation, if there is to be one, may not result solely from, and maybe not at all from, a resurgence of existing Reformational denominations, but rather may very well emerge from the reforming of the broader American pop evangelical church. There is evidence that this has already begun to happen to some degree with developments such as: the former Liberate organization and its progeny, the Gospel Coalition, the introduction of the New City catechism and the New Calvinists movement, a.k.a. the Young, Restless, and Reformed movement.[1] Additionally, the quality Reformational podcasts now available to the broader evangelical community, such as the *White Horse Inn* and *Issues, Etc.*, have been very helpful to many.

---

1. The latter is somewhat of a misnomer. Adopting limited aspects of Reformed theology such as the five points of Calvinism may arguably qualify one to use the label Calvinist to some extent, while the Reformed label should be reserved for those embracing the full substance of the Reformed confessions, i.e., either the Three Forms of Unity or the Westminster Standards.

16

More than a Message
Feasting on the Bread of Life

The sermon—the preaching of the Word—along with the sacraments, formed the heart of Reformational worship. We would call it a healthy gourmet cuisine. Back in the day, not being so health conscious, they would call it meat and potatoes. In any event, the feast was spread and it was substantial. The spotlight was on Christ and his redeeming work.

As the decades and centuries following the Reformation passed, this would not always be the case. And often, to continue the food metaphor, God's minister wasn't very Christ-like in waiting on tables. Sometimes he sounded more like a professor giving a lecture or a stern judge at a weekly parole hearing. Sometimes he forgot God was using him as an ambassador and thought that since the power was God's anyway, that he need not even try to communicate effectively. Sometimes the service sounded like a perpetual funeral. The transcendence and immanence of God portrayed in imbalanced ways often resulted in his gifts being distributed in the most distasteful of ways and sometimes not at all. This phenomenon would later give the contemporary church marketers a lot of traction (only to ultimately result in truly wild imbalances in the other direction). Another erroneous excess in many pop and Reformational evangelical churches was the diminishment of the sacrament of the Lord's Supper. This often resulted in its infrequent administration in church services. Like preaching was often reduced to mere teaching, communion was also often relegated to simply being a memorial as our means of commitment, rather than God's means of grace.

Generally, though, the old Reformational churches did understand that true joy does not emanate from the trivial. Church was not just another shopping mall. The preaching of the Word was not merely a lecture, but a dramatic event itself where God brought life and growth into being by his words. It was pedagogical and sacramental. Similarly, the Lord's Supper was not merely a memorial, but a foretaste of the feast to come, which effectually strengthened faith. Both were properly understood to be means of grace for the benefit of God's children. In communion, the gospel was visibly and tangibly proclaimed and the people were further fed and renewed. It was, and is, a union with, i.e., a participation in, the righteous body and blood of Christ (1 Cor 10:16).

The church was an empty tomb where the spiritually dead were brought to life with the further future hope of a bodily resurrection. It was a hospital where sinners were miraculously cured. It was criminal court where prisoners were taken off of death row. It was a civil court where orphans were adopted. It was a nursery where bruised reeds were transplanted so that they could thrive and bear fruit. It was an embassy of grace, part of a growing kingdom around the world. It was the residence quarters at the White House where the president enjoyed a meal with and fed his adopted children. It was a refreshing, cleansing fountain and pool. Not a mere auditorium or theatre, it was a sanctuary providing rest for the weary and heavy laden. More than a personal quiet time or family devotions, it was where the holy of holies was to be found—in the public gathering of the body at the Divine Service (Rom 10:6–8). It was Christmas and Easter all year round where his gifts of grace were ever being generously dispensed by the preaching of the gospel and the administration of the sacraments. It was to be both a serious place where God was worshipped in reverence and awe (Heb 12:28) and, though not always made apparent enough, a very happy place of unspeakable joy (Pss 42:4; 66:1; 100; 122:1; Luke 2:10; Rom 5:10–11; 1 Pet 1:8–9). It was in this place where the deepest root problems I could or would ever have—guilt and death—were completely resolved with good news beyond my wildest dreams.

The issue we face today is that there are two very different ways of conducting the service. On the one hand there is a tempting formula which will work, in that it will quickly draw a crowd. Basically you downplay humanity's serious sinful condition, stroke the egos of your hearers, provide practical tips for living (do more and try harder), incorporate them into a social structure and season it with entertaining and mystical pop music to create an exciting experience. Doing this will attract a crowd and may even fill stadiums. It will work and it will feel good for a time, but it is semi-pagan. It is cotton candy, and its sugar high can be fun, but it will not sustain for the long haul. Revivalistic movements will come and go. All of the hype over a movement in one era, such as Promise Keepers, will give way to a new hyped-up radical movement a few years later in a never-ending cycle in which people get burned out. In the end, there are casualties; there are people who become deluded as to what Christianity is all about and God's children, who do survive, are sadly short changed and sometimes sold short their whole life through.

On the other hand, there is an alternative to pandering to the sheep's proclivity toward legalism and mysticism. It is to richly nourish, bathe, and clothe God's children every week with the good news that "Jesus has come to do for us what we could never do for ourselves" and that "everything I need I already have in Christ."[1] It is in this environment that God's children do not just merely survive, but actually thrive. This is worship pleasing to God. It is modeled according to what he has revealed in his word and what he desires, not what we think it should be like. It's not about our doing or our experience. It's not another rock concert or sporting event. He doesn't tell us that he is a consuming fire who must be worshipped in awe and reverence to scare us. He is simply revealing to us the reality of his holiness and our unholiness. *God pleasing worship is where, in spite of this reality, he graciously descends and draws near to us through the ordinary means of preaching and sacraments to provide his wonderful gifts to us.* The service is primarily sacramental with his gifts coming down to us and secondarily sacrificial with our sacrifices/offerings of praise and thanksgiving going up to him. Here the word is rightly divided between law (diagnosis) and gospel (deliverance) with Christ at the center of all Scripture. Taking the preaching, baptizing and teaching directive of the Great Commission of Matthew 28 together with the teaching, fellowship, breaking of the bread, and prayers description of Acts 2, we have the delivery system God himself set up and reveals to us to deliver his promises. In this place we don't claim either "all this we will do" or, "have I not done?" It is here that he serves us and washes our feet. Here there is the objective certainty of his gifts being delivered to us according to his promises, not the uncertainty of what I

1. Tchividjian, "Jesus + Nothing = Everything," 189, 141.

might conjure up as my emotional "worship experience." This is the kind of worship he desires. We need to put aside our desire to have an experience and honor what he wants. We may just discover biblical worship to be more wonderfully experiential than anything we could have ever attempted or imagined.

No age on this earth is or will be a perfect golden age. There have been, however, at least two eras in the life of the church when the church has shone very, very brightly, despite its shortcomings: the early church and the Protestant Reformation. It was during both of those times when the doctrines of grace were clearly proclaimed and the gospel did its work. It is the gospel that creates and sustains faith. It alone is the power unto salvation. It alone creates true revival. The evangelical church needs to again feed the sheep richly with what they truly need, the Bread of Life. In so doing, they will be lifted up to new heights, heights higher than their basic instincts would have ever even dreamed of.

17

Transcendent and Immanent Equilibrium

The Geeky, Ultra-serious, Strange, Stoic, Lofty Syndrome

THE REFORMERS UNDERSTOOD THAT while God works through human means and that we are called to do our best in all things, he will accomplish his will. We need never worry. None of the elect will ever be lost due to our failures and no one can add to the elect by our zealous ingenuity. Therefore, most traditionalists properly understand that it is not right to pander to unbelievers (so-called "seekers") in the Divine Service, which, by design, exists to serve those who are redeemed and those who will be redeemed by God. Nonetheless, they often also make the serious mistake of defending certain practices that are not biblical and do not properly serve the redeemed. Maintaining pews without cushions, defending the joyless, crabby, monotone vocal delivery of their pastors, as well as enabling half-dead organ playing, are just a few. This brings us to another decline from the glories of the Reformation that is again often attributable to the traditionalists as much as it is due to the contemporary innovators—the delivery of the Divine Service.

In every area of life we quite rightly expect people to do their best while at the same time resting in God's sovereignty—except, that is, for traditional conservative preachers and their communication skills and characteristics. This group almost always gets a free pass when their work in delivering the goods is criticized or questioned. After all, the Apostle Paul made it clear that the gospel is effectual by God's power and not by human eloquence. True enough; however, there appears to be a cluster of off putting characteristics discussed below which are often associated with this type of preaching that goes far beyond a mere lack of eloquence. These characteristics can end up distorting the very message that God has revealed and wants conveyed. Consequently, Christians, being created in God's image, don't tolerate these accompanying characteristics for long. Very soon they end up seeking an alternative church. God has chosen to work through means using human instruments thereby intending to employ their humanity to its fullest. While legalism is responsible for much of the damage in historical Reformational churches, emotional detachment is not far behind.

We've previously alluded to this ongoing issue in traditional, conservative Reformational circles of the boring, stoic, 1950s-ish, lecture-like, funeral-like or probation hearing-like church service. There, even the psalms and hymns that are meant to be joyous expressions of praise are often played so slowly on the organ that they sound like funeral dirges. Preaching in such contexts is often also characterized by an antiquated loftiness from lips often surrounded by a historical looking beard. Defenders have posited that since the gospel is counterintuitive, i.e., strange and that which does not come naturally to us, the service ought to look strange. The problem is that this strangeness often goes far beyond the gospel and it is our self-created strangeness that becomes the offense rather than the gospel! It's also been argued by analogy that no one should complain when receiving a large gift of money from someone at a restaurant that happens to be an absolute dive; however, that is like saying we can model police academies after the habits of Inspector Clouseau! It's one thing to say that it may happen that way, but it's certainly not the ideal to shoot for. This would be like delivering the bread of life in the form of a hospital feeding tube packet handed to someone needing nourishment and believing that we've been faithfully diligent in delivering the goods.

How do we sort out this problem which we have entitled as a kind of syndrome? The Reformers distinguished between what Luther called the theology of the cross and the theology of glory. Essentially this distinction recognizes that God primarily works through suffering and means that look weak and foolish to us. A theology of glory, on the other hand, exalts

Transcendent and Immanent Equilibrium

man's wisdom and power and the means that we naturally think are effective. As stated above, the Apostle Paul makes this very point that the power of preaching is not in the preacher's speaking ability, but in the gospel being preached. Similarly, Scripture specifically notes Moses poor speaking ability and that of other leaders as well. For this reason it is prudent to concede and recognize that preaching in the most biblically faithful churches might well always be generally destined to be characterized by what we perceive as weak, geeky, poor public speaking abilities. The problem is that the geeky speaking often comes packaged with a lot of other baggage. While the geeky speaking part of this "syndrome" is defensible according to Scripture and perhaps inevitable, the ultra-serious, strange, stoic and lofty parts of this syndrome are not. These things, which distort the very message that we are trying to convey, can and should be rooted out and corrected. Congregants are often left with a service and a sermon that is overly heady and tedious.

No, the gospel's power is not about the eloquence of the minister or his personality, but often these other distorted characteristics are present as well. As a result, the message being conveyed can become distorted. These problems have not been adequately addressed in many smaller, conservative circles, creating stumbling blocks for the hearers. These issues continue to drive people away in such contexts, especially regenerated people! While such a minister's message may remain effectual, to be sure, it's only getting out to the three people left sitting in such a dwindling church! If people have a choice between Seinfeld's "Soup Nazi" and another chef serving substantially the same thing with joy and cheerfulness, they will opt for the latter. The same thing goes for picking a physician who has a good bedside manner over one who does not. This is basic to our humanity, which is created in God's image.

If the ambassador of the King is not communicating both the immanence (tender nearness) and transcendence (high majestic holiness) of God in a contemporary context, he is not faithfully proclaiming the Word as he ought. Many ministers are so transcendent, aloof and serious in conservative services that the people never can breathe and enjoy communion with their Father, who is called *Abba* (Mark 14:36; Rom 8:15; Gal 4:6). Yes, this is serious business. Yet, once the assurance of pardon is received there ought to be an immanent time enjoyed in the service when the ambassador is now in his role representing *Abba* Father. He then can, in fact, laugh, joke, and be casual to a degree, i.e., joyful as the Bread of Life is preached, in addition to, and in variation with, being serious. God loves a cheerful giver of the message of grace, not one who leaves the flock wallowing in the seriousness of their sinful condition. By not being faithful in this, we have only ourselves to blame for creating the huge backlash of immanence by the church marketing movement. By the way, this problem is greatly alleviated in churches which have maintained the historic liturgy, including the *Kyrie*, for that is customarily followed by a very joyous song, *to wit:* "Glory to God in the Highest" or "Worthy Is Christ (the Lamb)," a.k.a. "This Is the Feast of Victory for Our God." Consequently, there is a distinct transition in the mood of the service to that of great joy.

A minister of any speaking ability and of any personality can show both the role of a judge and a father. Being all transcendent in this culture is like doing the Mass in Latin and expecting the Holy Spirit to bless the effort. Often times, these ministers will use a lofty voice of proclamation throughout the entire service that is not only foreign to the culture, but hopelessly out of date for the church as well. This can be particularly true in many Reformed and Presbyterian circles where very plain and bland architecture often surrounds the pulpit/table/font—with maybe a plastic green plant and a flag or two in the background, just to make it look completely cheesy. Ministers then necessarily are trying to compensate with their voices to create a sense of transcendence and end up overcompensating. I think the beautiful, transcendent architecture more often found in Anglican and Lutheran churches, and the formality already made present by the more formal liturgies of these churches, gives the pastor the appropriate freedom to convey the immanence of God. He is not pressured in such a context to create transcendence. For example, having solemnly gathered as a people, made confession of sin, received a formal assurance of pardon, the people then stand up at attention (as when a judge enters the courtroom) to receive the formal greeting just prior to the preaching of the Word. Worship practices such as these already establish the requisite awe and reverence. In such a context, the minister is then free to convey the immanence of "Abba Father" and the joy that results. He does not have to try to sound like he thinks a Puritan or a solemn sixteenth-century king might have sounded. We do, in fact, have royalty in today's culture, but it is much more characterized by Prince William and Kate, Duchess of Cambridge, than by King Henry VIII!

Similarly, acoustic guitars often can better reflect immanent music than the organ. The pipe organ, the instrument with the greatest range of musical notes better reflects the transcendent. Because of that, many in the past have made the leap that all of the music must be high culture classical, which became exclusionary. As the old hymn says, "Let them [the common folk] praises give Jehovah!"[1] But neither is this to condone the poor lyrical and musical quality of much contemporary Christian pop music. On that side of the worship wars, the popular market driven forces at work in the preaching and singing in the renovated warehouses of many contemporary churches sacrifice far too much of the transcendence of God. Beside the total lack of transcendence in preaching and singing, the transcendent form and beauty of historic Christianity which characterizes the old church buildings is lost as well. Both the immanence and transcendence of God need to be conveyed in the service in the language of the people. It is, after all God's service. When it's all about us, like a wedding ceremony, for example, even suits and dresses are not enough. They give way to tuxedos and gowns; we don't hesitate to pour on the liturgy;[2] and, since few want to be married in a contemporary warehouse church in a business park, many love to find that quaint old church with beautiful architecture and stained glass windows to get married in.

In God's service, the truth always needs to be spoken in love in the context of present day culture. God is to be worshipped in awe and reverence, yet with the presence of joy. How we accomplish the appropriate balance of transcendence and immanence will vary. Within these parameters there are many issues which are simply preference issues. Different combinations of architecture, seriousness, speaking style, music and liturgy are a part of the diversity that makes up the family of God. Moreover, weekly liturgies can be varied somewhat among alternatives to ensure an appreciation for the historical elements of worship without falling into rote, mindless ritual. In the world, but not of the world; foreign, but not out of touch, are delicate touchstones to which we must aspire. In Old Testament worship where God's people were simultaneously beneficiaries of the Abrahamic covenant of grace, but also burdened as a nation with fulfilling the Mosaic covenant of works if they hoped to remain in the promised land, there was, understandably, much serious lament. In the new covenant, which is solely of grace, there still should be a time of confession and lament due to our ongoing sinfulness, though this will be less pronounced. Here the burden is quickly relieved inasmuch as we are again reminded that Christ has fulfilled the law on our behalf. In the end, the accent must fall where

---

1. William J. Kirkpatrick, "Hallelujah, Praise Jehovah," in *Psalter Hymnal*, no. 304.
2. See Rhode, "Gospel for Former [Pop] Evangelicals."

Rod Rosenbladt has properly placed it. When describing what the Divine Service is all about, he conveys the idea that it's really good news, happy news! "Take heart, my son, your sins are forgiven" (Matt 9:2b). "Take heart, daughter; your faith has made you well" (Matt 9:22).

18

Let the Little Children Come to Me, for to Such Belongs the Kingdom Of Heaven

A Pitch for Infant Baptism

WHILE DIE-HARD BAPTISTS MAY be tempted to skip this section, most Reformational Christians affirm the sacrament of infant baptism. Among the many biblical reasons for this is the fact that the sign of God's covenant promise was always given, not just to a man as an individual, but to the man as head of the household. Thereby, the entire household was incorporated, including the infant children of the household who would also receive the sign of the covenant. When believing Abraham was circumcised in the OT as a sign of God's gracious covenant, he was also directed to have his son and the males of his household immediately circumcised. From then on all Israelite boys were circumcised on the eighth day. It would have been incomprehensible for New Testament Jewish Christians to think that their infant sons, if not their daughters as well, would not receive the sign of the new covenant in view of God's previous dealings with them, literally over centuries. Besides, as an expansion of the Abrahamic covenant, this new covenant was to be even more inclusive. Second, we never read of any controversy concerning the sign of the covenant being taken away from infants. Had that happened, it certainly would have caused a huge controversy given the historical context. Third, the canon of Scripture was not concluded until the end of the first century and therefore there were several generations of children who grew up in Christian households during that time. Despite that fact, we read of no baby dedications taking place nor of any believer baptisms of covenant children. Finally, we have household baptism records going all the way back to Irenaeus in the second century. Irenaeus was a disciple of Polycarp who was a disciple of the Apostle John. We also have a clear historical record of the infant baptism of Origen in AD 180. Again, we have no record of any intervening controversy which would suggest that this was a change.

In any event, we do have agreement among the Reformational churches (including the Reformational Baptists) that baptism is primarily a means of grace and not primarily our means of commitment, even in the case of adult baptism. Baptism, generally, is viewed as an important sacrament in the life of the church. It is regularly celebrated by everyone collectively in the service and not relegated to a private swimming pool ceremony, as is often the case in contemporary pop evangelicalism. Reformational churches, except for the Baptists, also believe that it should be administered to children. As lambs born to the sheep in the sheepfold of the shepherd, they are to be marked with the sign of the New Covenant. Reformational churches substantially agree that the gospel promise of the Triune God in tangible, visible form should "drown" or be splashed upon the face of the little ones by name—a gift from him, like a personalized wedding invitation as opposed to a general invitation. To be sure, this gospel promise must be received by faith. Like the OT children of Israel who had the gospel preached to them in the wilderness, it had to be combined with faith (Heb 3), which is also a gift of God.

Now, here is where the Lutherans and the Reformed/Presbyterians/Anglicans part ways and the difference is really not all that difficult to understand. The Lutherans believe that besides the gospel promise, the new birth, which consists of the gift of new life and faith in Christ, is imparted to that child no later than when the sign is actually administered. The Reformed, etc., take the position that while baptism is an effectual means of grace and while the seed of the gospel promise is planted, the Holy Spirit may effectuate the new birth and the gift of faith at another time. They distinguish between the sign and the reality of which the sign testifies to. The actual regeneration and gift of faith to such a child might occur before, during or after the administration of the sign. It is viewed as akin to the general preaching of the gospel which is effectual where the Holy Spirit is operative in its application to one's heart. As the wind blows where it will, no one knows from where the Holy Spirit comes or goes (John 3:8). Thus, for the Reformed, in the administration of the sign, the child is baptized into the visible covenant (church) community to share in its many blessings, but, like in the OT with the sign of circumcision, not necessarily and ultimately into the true invisible people of God (Heb 4:2).

Lutherans counter that the Scriptures make no distinction between water baptism and Spirit baptism and that it is all bound up in the very personalized administration of the sacrament, i.e., both the gift of gospel promise *and* the gift of new life and faith. The Lutheran position is often referred to as baptismal regeneration. This is not always the best word to use for it because the Reformed do not deny that regeneration can take place during the administration of the sign. Moreover, it confuses the issue further because Roman Catholics believe in baptismal regeneration, but not in the same way. In the Catholic view, grace is infused like a substance at regeneration, but then gets lost in degrees by venial sins, and totally by mortal sins. One must then merit the replenishment of grace by meriting the merits of Christ. Justification before God does not happen until there is perfect sanctification. Saints then get to go to heaven. In the Reformational view, grace is imputed, specifically, the righteousness of God, so that there is immediate justification. In this view, where grace is not a substance, but rather is God's favorable disposition toward sinners on account of Christ, sinners get to go to heaven. Sanctification is distinguished, but not separated from justification. It is the fruit of the root of justification. It is the doing of good works because I am already accepted by God, not in order that I might be accepted by God.

So what about the baptized kids who rebel? The Lutherans and Reformed, consistent with their differing views on the sacrament of baptism, look differently at the verses in Matthew 13 about some seed dying out and the verses in Hebrews 6 about those who have once been enlightened, who have tasted the heavenly gift, but have fallen from the faith. Lutherans maintain that you can reject or "shipwreck" the faith given to you (1 Tim 1:19), which you once had, since this gift was given to you in baptism in addition to the gift of the gospel promise. The Reformed maintain that such a one falling away never had a true saving faith in the gospel given him or her, since Jesus has promised not to lose any of the ones given to him by the Father (John 6:39; 17:12; 18:9). This is an issue that after five hundred years has yet to be resolved between them.

If there is anything American pop evangelicals don't have a stomach for, it is any suggestion of baptismal regeneration. Not only is it antithetical to our human nature, it is particularly antithetical to Americans. The common practice of giving parents an unlit candle at pop evangelical baby dedications appears to be a direct reaction to the customary historical Lutheran practice of giving the parents a lit candle signifying the gift of their child's new life in Christ at baptism. Evangelicals need to beware, however, of accusing the Lutherans of saying we are "saved by baptism" as opposed to being "saved by grace alone through faith alone in Christ alone." Both are true (1 Pet 3; Eph 2:8–9) and it was the Lutherans (and later the Reformed) who were the champions of the latter, which became the slogan of the Reformation! We are saved by virtue of our baptism into Christ. That is clear. Again, the question becomes whether or not the sign of baptism always contains and conveys the full reality signified by the sign. Put another way; does the administration of the sacrament ensure the effective delivery of one gift or two gifts? Does it convey Christ and all his benefits or that plus the work of the Holy Spirit?

I realize there are Lutherans who grew up rotely being encouraged to "remember their baptism" like a superstitious good luck charm which led some to think that faith was not necessary. However, such an encouragement, when rightly understood, is actually a call to exercise one's faith, i.e., to embrace by faith the gospel promise of their baptism. As a young boy, I recall being reminded of God's promise to me in baptism by my mother to be a tremendous source of comfort when learning about the phenomena of demon possession and other terrors of the night. Infant baptism is a wonderful personalized gift of God to covenant children that ought not be denied to them by evangelicals. Evangelical churches ought to allow for the option of parents having their children baptized. Then evangelicals can encourage their children to embrace the gospel promise given them in their baptism by faith, without having to first try and solve the mystery of exactly when the Spirit gives each such a faith. In short, infant baptism is God's gift which he regards as very important. It is what it is, whether we make too much of it or too little of it. Like the leeway Anglicanism permits on this, for those not persuaded one way or the other as to the extent of its efficacy, there should be no need to bind their consciences. They ought not have to speculate beyond what has been clearly revealed and understood, even as the church at large continues to grapple with what has been revealed and not yet uniformly understood.

19

Creation, Vocation and the Two Kingdoms

Why Christians Can, and Should, Spend the Week as Chefs, Stockbrokers and Special Ops

REFORMATIONAL CHURCHES CONTINUE THE liturgical tradition of ending the Divine Service with the *bene* ("good") *diction* ("word") from God himself to encourage his pilgrims for the coming week. It is usually stated as "Go in peace" or a variation thereof. The people would be restored, fed, and equipped for another week of service to glorify God by loving and serving their neighbors in their various vocations and bearing witness to Christ and his gospel.

The Reformation-era Christians had a great understanding of the doctrine of creation, the two kingdoms[1] and vocation. Luther built upon Augustine's work in this area and the results were revolutionary. The Reformers understood that Jesus was Lord over the civil kingdom of this age ruling through common grace providence. This included all of the varied vocations given to people by a perfect Creator in a creation that was, though fallen, very good. All work was a calling of God. One no longer needed to

---

1. A number of the Reformed have consistently refrained from using the two kingdoms terminology. While recognizing the distinctions discussed here, they do not draw as sharp of a divide as do the Lutherans and other Reformed. They prefer to speak of one kingdom having different dimensions, but with much more overlap than the two kingdoms approach would suggest.

be a monk or a priest to be fully validated in serving. As citizens of the civil kingdom, we are all given the cultural commission to fulfill (Gen 1:28) as well as the Great Commandment to live by—to love God and our neighbor as ourselves (Matt 22:34–40). Moreover, they knew Christ was also Lord of that other kingdom, the coming kingdom, the kingdom of heaven, ruling through his special grace freely given by the preaching of the gospel and the administering of the sacraments.

As the centuries passed following the Reformation, the medieval (and similar Anabaptist) idea of exalting church workers over secular workers would reemerge. Though Reformational Christians would sometimes later be erroneously accused of being lukewarm and too worldly minded, they were right to vigorously serve their neighbors in their various common grace callings (1 Thess 4:11–12; Col 3:23) as providentially ordained by God. (A distortion of this teaching would later come to be known as the Protestant work ethic.) It is true that by the nineteenth and twentieth centuries many Reformational Christians deserved this criticism to some degree as they could have done a better job in America as far as bearing witness to Christ and his gospel. After all, while church planting is largely the job of missionaries, all Christians should be "evangelical" in readily sharing the reason for their hope. They did strongly support mission endeavors and their local churches, but their own churches often became clubs for succeeding generations, not very open and welcoming places for those outside. Granted, as we have previously observed, many of them were prone to introversion as many themselves were immigrants trying to cope in a new land. It was largely left to Wesley and the revivalists to evangelize the frontier, while Episcopalians and Presbyterians often stagnated. This sin also would eventually give the up and coming church marketing moguls a lot of fodder off of which to feed beginning in the 1970s. Christians always need to remember that beside the cultural commission and great commandment we have as individuals, the church, as an institution, has a great commission. Individual members of the church should actively share in that commission as well by witnessing in their spheres of influence in addition to supporting the local church and foreign missionaries.

Today in pop evangelicalism, the service rarely ends with a benediction sending people out with a clear understanding of vocation. The person on the barstool usually just says, "Dismissed." Pop evangelicals often start a week of busy "Christian" activities on top of their jobs and callings as spouses, parents and members of a local community. The medieval and

CREATION, VOCATION AND THE TWO KINGDOMS

Anabaptist exaltation of "Christian" work over "secular" work is back in full force. If one's job is not in missions, youth ministry or relief work, many feel like a second class Christian trying to compensate. This is because today's evangelical mindset steeped in Anabaptist separatist fundamentalism has no concept of the two kingdoms described above. Here there is only the kingdom of heaven, i.e., the Christian subculture and everything else on earth "out there" is seen as evil. The legitimacy of the civil kingdom, governed by God's providence, is not recognized. *Consequently, one's world is falsely limited to two categories: the sacred and the profane. Pop evangelicalism makes no room for the third category, for good things commonly and providentially provided for all in God's good creation, like our many and varied vocations.* So jobs become disconnected from one's faith and sort of meaningless, except, as a necessary evil, they put bread on the table. Christians often end up retreating from the "profane" culture into their little "holy" or "sacred" subcultures, not entirely unlike the Amish. Quaint? Perhaps, but such a lifestyle is not very helpful in defending against ISIS or producing pain medications like Novocain!

Other evangelicals, like myself, have suffered through the opposite response to this distorted categorization of reality—an extreme "transforming the world" paradigm. Though this paradigm has been around for a while in Reformed and Presbyterian circles in a more legitimate limited form, it has more recently taken a life of its own, particularly in emerging and emergent contexts. The idea taught here is not retreat or isolation. It is that everything not sacred—both profane and common—are to be redeemed and made sacred by us as God's agents in the world. While our being salt in serving our neighbors certainly can have transformative effects, especially when it comes to the profane things, many end up hopelessly trying to transform the world and all of its "common" things through their jobs with way over realized expectations. Instead, we ought to simply focus upon loving and serving our neighbors and leave it to God to usher in the new heavens and earth.

I recall the extreme frustration I felt as a young lawyer that I wasn't transforming the culture like I'd been taught to expect. Real estate closings and court appearances seemed far too mundane and worldly. If I wasn't in the ministry, then, at the very least, I should have been working to overthrow cases like Roe v. Wade. *It was as if the extraordinary endeavor would elevate the common vocation into something sacred and "kingdom-building."* Today, a "mission" trip to Thailand to rescue teenage prostitutes during your vacation is the expectation if an evangelical lawyer wishes to baptize one's law practice and validate themselves to the evangelical world as "holy."

My father, and many I observed of his ("greatest") generation, on the other hand, were more steeped in the doctrine of vocation and never seemed to have such discontent—and he was a watchmaker and jeweler! It always amazed me to think how falsely profane his good and common secular vocation would have been viewed as a logical consequence in the minds of many gnostic/Anabaptist-leaning evangelicals, at least as an unspoken assumption. But he properly never saw it that way. He knew that God created a world where there would be exquisite timepieces, both clocks and watches, gold rings to signify marital unions and stunning diamonds and gems gracing us with tiny glimpses of the glories of the new heavens and the new earth. And his jewelry repair bills for widows generally came to about two dollars. I, too, later learned that it was precisely in serving and loving my neighbor in my secular profession that one of my most important callings was realized. A multitude of files closed with thank you notes from people I had the privilege of helping made it clear that all of that prior frustration was very unnecessary and that there was nothing mundane about it. Such false thinking only arises from the distorted medieval gnostic mentality (grace vs. nature instead of grace vs. sin) and the radical Anabaptist (separatist) mindset, both so pervasive in modern American evangelicalism. Correcting this in contemporary evangelicalism would solve a lot of career frustration.

Therefore, as a result of being immersed in this false mindset, some, on the one hand, withdraw from society. There is no real time for your neighbors because the Christian separatist subculture has so many busy things for you do to. Saturated in "Christian" radio, some are no longer even aware of what's happening in the larger culture. Many become deprived of superior quality music (and theology) as well as other art forms and disciplines. On the other hand, feeling pressured to ascend to a higher realm by doing, not the ordinary, but the extraordinary things, others vainly try to transform the good and common into the holy and sacred. Eventually, burnout sets in and many Christians fall off the radar as the statistics sadly reveal. This is another example where we have not only largely failed in churching the unchurched, but are actually unchurching the churched. Evangelicals need to avoid both extremes of separatism and thinking they can build God's kingdom by transforming the culture. There is a paradox of Christ's lordship over both the kingdom of heaven and the civil kingdom. We are

Creation, Vocation and the Two Kingdoms

citizens of both and live in a tension between this age and the age to come, the "already" and the "not yet." We will have some transformative effect as salt and light in this passing age, but only he will usher in the age to come. How we relate to culture is also closely related to one's view of eschatology, which is the study of "last things" or "end times."[2]

In the meantime, it is for freedom that he has set us free. *Beside the "holy," we are free to enjoy all of the good and common gifts of creation God has given to believers and unbelievers alike* (Matt 5:45; 1 Tim 6:17). As we bear witness to the hope we have in Christ, God gave us mountains to ski, waters to sail, wines to sample, cuisines to taste, gardens to tend, many genres of music to listen to and multiple vocations whereby we can serve one another's needs. He providentially provides for our needs as neighbors serve one another in our many and varied callings. There are spouses to love. There are children to nurture. There are farmers to grow the grain, bakers to bake it, truckers to transport the bread, stores to dispense it, hairstylists to cut our hair, doctors to heal, accountants to help us account, artists to enrich our lives, teachers to teach, police to maintain safety, fire fighters to protect us, and travel guides to help arrange for times of recreational rest. Jesus himself validated and blessed vocation by, among other things, spending most of his perfect life working as a carpenter. The providential care that he has designed into the creation in this vast array of vocational service for us continues in spite of humanity's fall into sin and the resulting fallen world in which we find ourselves. God's providence is yet another amazing gift from the one who is "the overflowing fountain of all good."[3]

---

2. See Riddlebarger, *Case for Amillennialism*.
3. Belgic Confession of Faith, art. I; see also arts. XII and XIII.

PART 3

Some Additional Liberating Applications and Implications

20

The Railroad, AT&T and the Mega Church

Having looked at some foundational principles which we need to recover, then walking through the elements of the church service, we now turn our attention to some additional liberating applications and implications of some other Reformational, biblical truths, both for the life of the church and for the life of the Christian.

Today we assume the mega growth of churches as the ideal, both as to numbers and rate of growth. This was not always so. From both the Old Testament prophets and Jesus sermon in John 6 onward, it was never about attracting crowds or money, but about the faithful preaching of the Word. Generally speaking, the churches of the Reformation deliberately kept the size of their churches in check. When a church started to get too large, say beyond a couple hundred people, they would seed or plant a daughter church nearby. One can see in any American town or city, old modest sized church buildings in each neighborhood there to serve its little flock, i.e., a parish or congregation. This, the Reformers believed, followed the biblical pattern of the apostles going out and establishing new churches where a group of local elders, including a teaching elder or pastor, would be appointed and a church established before they moved on. This, in turn, followed the early Jewish pattern of establishing synagogues when there were ten men, i.e., heads of households available to do so. This was not because these churches didn't know how to be cool and get a good praise band to draw the crowds in, had they wanted to.

Part 3: Some Additional Liberating Applications and Implications

The church marketing movement set out to change all that. Applying business marketing principles to church growth, the old mom and pop parish sized churches were seen as obsolete, much like the old mom and pop grocery stores, shoe stores, etc., that filled Main Street America and that were traded in for the mall. The problem is that God's economy for building his church is different than the American business economy. When we try to import principles which are in conflict with the principles given to us in Scripture, a host of problems are not far behind. Departing from *sola Scriptura*, i.e., Scripture alone where Scripture has clearly spoken, is never a good idea. Moreover, even in the commercial economy, not everything falls into the mall or Walmart model. As Todd Wilken put it: "We would never say that there [should] be a town of ten thousand people with only one doctor . . . or with only one guy pumping gas."[1] Moreover, the new buzzwords "fastest growing" which are used to describe the latest mega phenomenon doesn't exactly match Scripture's description of sustained growth. There the seeds without roots, which sprout up quickly, end up dying (Matt 13:1–9; Mark 4:1–9; Luke 8: 4–15). Fast growth should never be exalted as a virtue in and of itself. Horton has observed that cancer often grows much faster than children do. Likewise, forest fires grow really fast. Ideologies such as fascism and Nazism can take hold of a culture overnight. *Putting the church on steroids by injecting the Druckerite principles of the church marketers may not be so healthy after all.*[2]

God has provided pastors, under-shepherds to care for his flock. In order to do that, they have to be able to know their flock. Being a CEO of a large megachurch simply does not allow for that to happen. Moreover, a monopoly is created for the whole geographic region covered by the megachurch along with all of the dangers that result from monopolies. This is further exacerbated by the current trend of multi-siting with one church establishing multiple campuses under its jurisdiction. This also does not follow the biblical and Reformational model of each church being governed by its own elders and pastor. As we have seen, it is basically creating an evangelical version of an archdiocese with the megachurch pastor setting himself up as the archbishop.

---

1. Wilken, "Listener Email and the Issues Etc. Comment Line, 11/1/12."

2. See Nesch, "Church of Tares." While I do not agree with everything that is stated in this documentary, it does provide a wealth of important information for the church to ponder.

The Railroad, AT&T and the Mega Church

Should there then be some serious dismantling and downsizing? What have the megachurches themselves done to deal with all of this? Small groups. Dare we tread upon this sacred cow of American pop evangelicalism?

21

Neither Lone Ranger nor Cultish Commune

The Abuse of Small Groups and the Communion of Saints

As American pop evangelicalism got into the mega business, there had to be a way to manage the large crowds in an orderly fashion. The basic building block for many megachurches is the small group. The idea of the small group was not new. John Wesley utilized them early on, drawing from the practice begun by a Lutheran named Philipp Jakob Spener who was influential in the Pietist movement. Spener's small groups were known as conventicles, little churches within the church. It was separate from the Word and Sacrament ministry of the church. As is often the case today, it was commonly (and wrongly) assumed that this is where the real action happened. As set forth in the Introduction above, the current small group movement received its impetus from management expert and social engineer, Peter Drucker, and has been a key component of the church marketing movement. Both Bill Hybels and Rick Warren were heavily influenced by Drucker's thinking. Both regard him as their mentor.

There have always been small groups of people in churches organizing for any number of activities such as Bible studies, fellowship, service projects, etc.; however, this was different in at least three ways. This was a deliberate sociological tool, in many cases, designed to manipulate the

Neither Lone Ranger nor Cultish Commune

crowd. Rick Warren is often quoted for the proposition that "small groups are the most effective way of closing the back door of your church"[1] thereby effectively keeping people from leaving. The social structure creates a certain peer pressure. Today in many pop evangelical churches, small group membership is not an option but a *de facto* requirement. If you wish to be regarded as spiritual, you must join and perhaps lead a small group. Often, those resistant to joining a small group are put on a guilt trip. *Doing life together in this way has become a new legalism.*

The now popular quip often made by small group promoters is that there's no such thing as a lone ranger Christian. I don't ever recall anyone in the past ever saying that Christians should be lone rangers. Sometimes there were, simply due to circumstances. I think of the Apostle John on the island of Patmos, or the Apostle Paul in a Roman prison, for instance. No, the gathering of the community for worship, fellowship and sharing have always been important and integral goals of the church; however, anything bordering on cult-like commune practices was never legitimately part of the church's enterprise.

Many churches now have elaborate hierarchical reporting systems to manage and monitor what is occurring in these groups led by lay small group leaders. Far too many of these groups are functioning in a manipulative peer pressure capacity creating yet another treadmill of performance. This can be particularly acute for people who are simply, by personality, not as social as others. For years, standardized personality tests have distinguished between people who find socializing to be energizing and those who find it to be draining. *Much like equating high-energy busyness with spirituality, equating a predilection for being really social with spirituality can be devastating to individuals less socially inclined and it is completely unbiblical.* How many have been driven away from the church by this mindset?

The covenant community is made up of all kinds of individuals who contribute in a variety of ways. It ought never to be given even the appearance of being limited to social butterflies who enjoy meeting weekly in each other's living rooms. Those who do enjoy that practice and are edified by it should continue, provided it is a truly voluntary option. Many have been deeply enriched by small group experiences within the church. Various groups organizing and getting together for various reasons have long been a vital part of the fellowship of believers in the church. On the other

---

1. Warren, "Relationships Hold Your Church Together," http://www1.cbn.com/biblestudy/relationships-hold-your-church-together.

hand, forcing people to do too much life together can be unhealthy for many individuals. It can also turn the church into a busy subculture where no one has the time to do life out in the world—precisely where Christians are desperately needed to be salt and light in their various callings. To whatever degree it is intentional, there is some wacky and manipulative social engineering going on in the name of community.

A second problem that we often find today is that these groups can be completely programmatic. Usually they are imposed organizationally. They generally do not arise from any kind of organic, natural or spontaneous fellowship as often happened in the older churches. Part of this, no doubt, is generational. Prior generations had little organized activities and playtime. They grew up using their own imagination and initiative and engaged in their own games of cops and robbers and pick-up basketball. The more recent generations following the baby boomers increasingly were brought up with organized activities and playtime. They were brought to an organized playtime, to organized sports practices and to organized music lessons. As a result, younger generations tend to be less spontaneous when it comes to social interaction. It's almost like the teacher or the coach is saying, "Okay children, small group time, now it's time to be authentic and transparent with one another."

Finally, and most importantly, *the Bible does establish an institution of small groups when it comes to what constitutes the building blocks for the church. It is called the family.* The leaders or shepherds of these groups are ideally two parents. The family has been instituted by God as a safe place for those being nurtured and where respect for the rights and dignity of each individual is fostered. These are the building blocks that God primarily has used to build his church throughout history. In fact, the breakdown of the family structure, both through divorce and the decline of extended family gatherings, has no doubt fueled the appeal for alternative small groups beginning with the generation that grew up on the television sitcom *Friends*. With more broken homes and "latchkey" kids, there is a greater hunger among many for more authority structure and community (which vulnerabilities are ripe for exploitation). As we have seen, the entity God primarily deals with is not first the individual, but the household or family unit. Pastors have the shepherding responsibilities for the larger collection of these families, including single parent families. Nowhere in Scripture are these pastoral responsibilities to be delegated to middle-level lay managers. Churches need to curb practices which constantly divide family members from each other and begin to re-engender a healthy respect for the family unit. Children have parents who are first and foremost responsible before God for their spiritual well-being. Young people ought never to be targeted as pawns of the mega pastor's latest "vision" for the church of the "new generation." Many megachurches intentionally and rigorously target the young people of a community. The resulting title wave of divisive pressure often inflicted upon families, where parents are trying to raise their children in the small church up the street, has been completely out of line.

The problem is that the current small group movement arises not out of the Bible, but out of the philosophy of Peter Drucker. His is a communitarian philosophy which some would say is a very dangerous one, due to its association with some of the elements of fascism.[2] As a result, there is a constant effort to biblically justify what is really the superimposing of a philosophy on Scripture. I can recall no other subject where there has been so much distorted exposition of Scripture to make it about something that it's not about. *If you listen to the preaching in many megachurches, it would now seem that half of the Bible is about organized small groups! Who knew?!*

While at first it might feel cool to be led by a cool looking dude in informal worship which is devoid of formalities such as God's greeting and benediction, there is the potential for great danger in such settings. When the office of minister as the King's ambassador and as the under-shepherd of Christ is diminished, two things happen. *When the Reverend or the Pastor becomes Bob, my buddy and comrade, a vacuum is created for both vision and authority.* The King's vision gets usurped by Bob's vision casting. The King's authority gets usurped by "leaders" or, to put it in Peter Drucker's native language, "führers." Hence, we now have the contemporary job description of a pastor, not as the servant of Christ, but as the "vision casting leader" who becomes empowered with cadres of small group leaders to promote his "vision." What often initially happens is that he receives a (scandalous) salary clothed in secrecy. Instead of humbly submitting and welcoming correction from a true body of independent elders, the elders often are his pawns, while the people are continually warned that they dare not criticize him or the church. And so the downward spiral goes in far too many cases.

If there is going to be a valid case made for the long-term continuation of the megachurch, there are going to have to be some adjustments. It may not always be healthy for such a large group of people to always be hearing

---

2. See Rosebrough, "Resistance Is Futile."

the Word preached from just one preacher. There may have to be some intentional variety in the weekly preaching. There needs to be additional professional pastoral care pastors to reclaim some, if not most, of the pastoral responsibilities that have been abdicated to the lay small group leaders. Families and individuals need to be respected as families and individuals, with their rights and dignity not being sacrificed in a sea of "community." The organizational legalism needs to end and people again need to be given the freedom to be spontaneous. The older churches that had a Sunday evening service were often criticized for legalistically expecting attendance at this second service. In my experience, the legalistic expectations for small group attendance has far exceeded whatever legalistic expectations formerly existed in the older churches that had Sunday evening services. Perhaps reinstating the Sunday evening service periodically as a voluntary optional opportunity for more grace on this day of rest might be a good substitute for some of the current small group activity. It might help avert some unhealthy inward directed focus and actually restore a more Christ centered focus. As the old churches would often beautifully sing in concluding this time of "evensong": "Savior, Again to thy dear name we raise, with one accord our parting hymn of praise . . . with Thee began, with Thee shall end the day."[3] Sunday was and is, after all, the Lord's Day.

---

3. John Ellerton, "Savior, Again to Thy Dear Name We Raise," in *Psalter Hymnal*, no. 326.

22

The Way Forward
Ice Cubes or Icebergs?

USING ICE AS AN analogy for talking about denominations is a little unusual—unless you are joking about them. Members of the very conservative small Reformational denomination known as the Orthodox Presbyterian Church are sometimes affectionately referred to as the "frozen chosen" for their sometimes less than user-friendly ways and shortcomings in effective outreach. Be that as it may, I think the ice metaphor can be especially appropriate in this age of spiritual global warming.

We have previously identified the major Reformational traditions and their respective confessions. We have further observed that there is much more overlap in these traditions than difference. The Reformation was not perfectly united and therefore there were a few giant, yet distinct icebergs, *to wit*: Lutheran, Anglican/Episcopalian, Presbyterian/Reformed, Congregationalist, and Baptist. Beside the Roman Catholic departures from sound doctrine at the Council of Trent where key teachings of the Reformation were condemned, there were also some fissures in the hoped for catholic unity of the churches of the Reformation as well. The denominations did, in fact, unite large numbers of churches on a worldwide scale. The unity achieved by the major denominations was remarkable, yet proximate and not universal in scope. Even on the Roman Catholic side, while there is enforced organizational unity which gives the appearance of catholicity, there has, in fact, always been *de facto* fissures there as well. The unity of Christ's church is surely an ideal not yet perfectly realized.

Part 3: Some Additional Liberating Applications and Implications

American pop evangelicalism, despite its protestations against denominational division, has done more to promote disunity than any other movement. We now have a plethora of denominations. The explosive growth of denominations has been, in large part, simply due to one group of Christians trying to distinguish themselves as being "holier" than the group from whom they were separating. On top of that we have countless ice cubes known as nondenominational churches where each have their own little unique statement of faith and no accountability beyond themselves to the church at large. The contemporary evangelical legacy has had a much more divisive than unifying effect.

In order to change, the multitude of ice cubes needs to start coming together. True unity is always rooted in Christ and his Word. It is the departures from sound teaching that actually cause sinful division of the unity of the body of Christ (Rom 16). For some five hundred years now, and over several continents, we have general agreement on basic teachings of Scripture as set forth in the vast overlapping portions of the major Reformational confessions. Furthermore, where Lutherans and Reformed have worked together, each has discovered even more commonality with the other's confession than they realized existed. Working together, both end up more biblically balanced. Sometimes, certain truths have become buried in one's own confession simply due to certain emphases having been placed on other truths over long periods of time. It is time for the American pop evangelical churches to unite in all of these overlapping and common areas. Without attempting all at once to resolve the remaining differences in the confessions, this would be a significant historical step for the church to grow in maturity and move forward toward unity in Christ and his Word. Even the creation of another confessional denominational identity to effectuate such a purpose would not divide further, but would, in fact, provide a forum for multiple ice cubes to coalesce around God's word. It would distinctly increase the unity for which Jesus prayed for us. *For those beginning to embrace the truths recovered during the Reformation, but not ready to completely embrace either the Reformed or Lutheran side of the Reformation, there needs to be a Reformational evangelical option which is clearly distinct from the current genres of American pop evangelicalism.*

By way of illustration, areas of agreement arising out of the Reformation confessions, as a whole, could include the five *solas* of the Reformation: salvation by grace alone, through faith alone, in Christ alone, as revealed in Scripture alone, to the glory of God alone. It could include humankind's total depravity and God's election of the redeemed. It could include the criteria for what constitutes a church. It could include the Divine Service, the law-gospel distinction and the three uses of the law as they relate to the gospel. It could include the power and objectivity of the gospel. It could include the passive and active obedience of Christ. It could include our passive and active righteousness. It could include the doctrines of creation and vocation. It could include so many riches of solid biblical teaching that were recovered in the Reformation. Churches would no longer have to waste time reinventing wheels and would be free to live and serve in light of the vast treasures left to them by prior generations of believers through the work of the Holy Spirit.[1]

As to some of the differences, what has happened in the past is that denominations sadly often became identified solely by their differences, i.e., either their church government or the unique teachings in their confessions. On the Reformed or Calvinist side of the Reformation, Episcopalians, Presbyterians and Congregationalists partly brought this upon themselves from the outset by making their form of church government their identity. Congregationalists are governed solely on the local level. Presbyterians are governed by local presbyters or elders, yet are part of, and subject to, broader assemblies. Episcopalians are governed by the *episcopus*, the bishop. In terms of theology, evangelicals have sometimes found it difficult to swallow a particular Calvinistic or Reformed teaching. As a result many other great Calvinist and Reformed teachings have also been ignored and have gone by the wayside.

On the Lutheran side, the Lutheran Church (Missouri Synod) is an example of a church that tends to be identified by others based upon a few unique teachings as well. Much, if not most, of the content of this book consists of the wonderful biblical teachings that the LCMS has emphasized and continues to faithfully teach (i.e., the Divine Service, the law/gospel distinction, vocation, etc.). While these teachings are shared throughout the Reformational denominations, there are a few distinct teachings in the LCMS, that most of today's evangelicals find difficult to accept. Since evangelicals in the past have tended to focus on these differences in a reactionary sort of way, the costly price was that all of the other great influences we find in confessional Lutheranism were also ignored and eventually lost in contemporary evangelicalism.

---

1. See Palmer, *Holy Spirit*, 160–63.

Part 3: Some Additional Liberating Applications and Implications

What then should evangelicals do with the differences? We have already discussed in some depth above, one of these differences: infant baptismal regeneration. Due in some measure to reactionary responses, infant baptism itself has fallen by the wayside in most contemporary evangelical churches. For the reasons discussed above, infant baptism ought to and can be recovered without evangelicals thinking they need immediately resolve the now centuries-old issue reflected in the Reformed vs. Lutheran position on the regeneration question. Furthermore, at the very least, parents ought to be given the option to baptize their children who can then profess their faith at a later time. Unless a church is taking a stand as a Baptistic church, evangelical churches that don't wish to impose infant baptism on its members, should also not impose a prohibition on parents who do wish to have their covenant children baptized.

Another significant difference is the Lutheran belief in the bodily presence of Jesus in and with the elements of communion (sometimes referred to as consubstantiation). While distinguishable from the Roman Catholic doctrine of transubstantiation, this view, nonetheless, is also distinguishable from the Calvinistic Reformed/Presbyterian view of Christ's presence in the sacrament received by faith as opposed to the presence in the elements. The Reformed maintain that the bodily resurrected Jesus is seated at the right hand of the Father and that his attribute of omnipresence of his divine nature does not cross over into his human nature. Lutherans, on the other hand, point to the miracle of Jesus changing the water into wine and also the feeding of the five thousand with five loaves and two fish as preparing the church for this ongoing miraculous physical event. The Reformed counter that Jesus words "this is my body" when he broke the bread in the institution of the Lord's Supper are not meant to create a quagmire of metaphysical, philosophical speculation for the church. They maintain that these words instead should be understood in light of the covenantal coordinates of Scripture. Michael Horton explains:

> For secular backgrounds to the biblical concept, we have to return to the world of ancient Near Eastern treaty making, as in the Hittite example, where, "This is the head of Mati'ilu and his son" is explained by the suzerain as the assumption of the treaty's obligations and curses for violation. In the ceremony it is announced that the severed head of the goat is no longer a mere goat's head but the head of Mati'ilu and his sons . . . , covenantal actions are not merely illustrations [symbolic]. Yet they are also not a magical [or, presumably, miraculous] transformation of earthly substances

into divine substances. Rather, they are performative actions that do what they say. In and through the act of consecrating bread and wine as his body and blood, Jesus hands himself over to death as the sacrifice for the sins of those who eat and drink in faith. He offers them the "cup of salvation" because he will drink the "cup of wrath" to its dregs . . .[2]

There is clear agreement that communion is a sacrament (gift from God) to nourish and strengthen faith. Both groups properly maintain that in partaking the bread and wine, there is an actual participation in the body and blood of Christ. It is a celebration of our union with Christ. For both, it is a remembrance of his passion (the altar connotation) and it is also a foretaste of the heavenly feast he is preparing (the Lord's Table connotation). It is not merely an ordinance (law) to commemorate a memorial feast that we perform, which is what most pop evangelicals have tried to reduce it to.

Again, this is another area where evangelicals can at least unite on these points where there is agreement among all the Reformational denominations, without attempting to immediately resolve what large groups of Lutherans and Reformed have been unable to resolve over five hundred years. (The resolution ultimately could be more of a both/and answer rather than an either/or answer, particularly in light of the Lord's Supper constituting an in breaking of the age to come where there will be no separation between earth and heaven.) As in the case of infant baptism, it would be a step forward to a least coalesce around where we have consensus and leave solving the mystery part for another day. This is not at all to say that the confessional Reformed and Lutheran denominational positions should not continue for those who subscribe, and for those who will wish to subscribe. Many on both sides are fully convinced as to what they believe, teach and confess concerning their respective confessions including their respective details, some of which are very lengthy and detailed. Though they all can't be right, many of those details may well be right.[3]

2. Taken from *The Christian Faith* by Michael Horton. Copyright © [2011 by Michael Horton]. Use by permission of Zondervan. www.zondervan.com. 781–82. See also chs. 23 & 24, esp. 798ff.

3. To be sure, there are other long-standing differences among the major Reformational denominations as well. For example, while all try to be sacramental and catholic, the Lutherans and Anglicans believe in the normative principle of worship. Worship practices are thus normed by Scripture in the sense that they reject anything contrary to Scripture. Things not specifically prohibited in Scripture are thus permitted. They permit candles in worship, whereas the Reformed generally do not. Images and pictorial representations of Jesus are also permitted, whereas they are generally not permitted in

PART 3: SOME ADDITIONAL LIBERATING APPLICATIONS AND IMPLICATIONS

On the other hand, it would seem that there is also room for a shorter Reformational confession (and denominational identity) at this particular time in history. Given the lack of consensus on some of these issues for five hundred years, it would seem foolish to expect all evangelicals to have to make commitments on these issues at this time in order to return to being Reformational. Anglicanism does provide this option to a degree, but its confession is perhaps too short. Arguably, it could be said that the brevity of its confession continues to contribute to its lack of consensus and liberal decline, at least in the West. *One way or another, an alternative evangelical option is needed, if for no other reason than providing a broadly accessible and significant stepping stone to reformation.* Requiring all evangelicals to adhere to every detail of one confession or the other as they currently exist would unnecessarily bind the consciences of many. In the meantime, let the discussions and debates go on. No doubt, hardcore Lutherans and hardcore Reformed will both say I have only taken the reader 80 percent "there," i.e., toward a new reformation. I agree that all evangelicals, along with Lutherans and the Reformed, need to work on the remaining 20 percent where there are differences, according to the grace given us. It might just prove helpful to the church to have a generation of theologians, whose pensions are not tied to their subscription to one confession or the other, working on these issues. Just sayin'... They could end up affirming either camp as they now exist or perhaps move us forward toward reconciliation in some of these areas where there are differences. In the meantime, let us move things forward on the 80 percent areas of agreement and pray that the Holy Spirit would continue to guide and grow the church as biblical scholarship in these remaining areas matures more and more. "Christ promised that the Spirit of truth would guide the church into all truth (John 16:13)."[4] Let the truth be spoken in love to one another that the whole body may be built up and grow in the grace and knowledge of our Savior, Jesus Christ (Eph 4:15; 2 Pet 3:18). As we continue to work these things out with much prayer, let

---

Reformed sanctuaries, due in part to a differing interpretation of the second commandment. The Reformed, on the other hand, believe Scripture teaches a regulative principle of worship in which only that which is commanded/described in Scripture is allowed. Thus the Reformed theoretically allow for less freedom in worship practices. The Lutheran/Anglican respect for catholicity, history and tradition on the other hand produce an end result not all that different. Another difference is a sermon which is often in the nature of a short homily, as opposed to the more lengthy and expository preaching of the Reformed, which unfortunately usually results in one extreme or the other for both groups!

4. Palmer, *Holy Spirit*, 160.

us all look forward to that day when we will behold Christ, 100 percent, in all of his glory.

On an added note, in my experience, even where people can agree with the confession of a Reformational church, often there are practices in the church which drive them away. We have already looked at the stoic practice of curbing all expressions of joy present in many traditional church services. Another practice in many Reformed churches is to so emphasize the study of the Word, that their practice of having lengthy morning and evening services in addition to a Sunday school education hour become a legalistic burden. While it may not always be intended as such, attendance at all of these often becomes an expectation and a *de facto* requirement of good standing in the church. This practice seems to work well with Ivy League types, other intellectually disposed people and the average person who is good at daydreaming their way through. It simply has not always been healthy for the average person on the street. By way of analogy, even those who enjoy a good steak would find back to back visits to a steakhouse on the same day hard to digest As a result, many people of average intelligence, who would otherwise identify as Reformational, end up in pop evangelicalism. Even some who are content with these practices for themselves, will seek alternatives for their teenage children and other people they might invite to church. A Reformational evangelical alternative with a less rigorous church order and practice would therefore provide a much needed option for many. Moreover, there is a wealth of good Reformational material now available in print and online to supplement discipleship (teaching) where there is a single weekly service.

We must take care not to checkmate people out of Reformational Christianity. This can happen by insisting upon immediate adherence to a confession that, for some, is simply overly detailed. It can also happen by virtue of insisting on practices which people of varying dispositions will find overly restrictive and confining. If existing evangelical churches made the types of changes we have discussed, large numbers of emerging Reformational evangelicals could be accommodated. These churches could then coalesce together in a monumental step forward and perhaps even begin a new era in the history of the church. *We desperately need in evangelicalism an infusion of churches that are Reformational, sacramental and mission-minded, which are neither stoic and legalistic, nor based upon a seeker driven entertainment/small group megachurch model.*

23

Getting from Happy Meals to the Healthy Plate

Hypocrisy and Other Hurdles

THERE IS A MAJOR paradigm shift now taking place in the American diet. New generations are being educated in healthy nutrition from infancy and older generations are slowly getting it. The shift from a meat and potatoes / burger and fries paradigm is very slowly and finally giving way to a healthier diet. From the USDA's "Food Pyramid" followed by "My Plate," to Harvard's "Healthy Eating Plate," to Jamie Oliver's "Food Revolution," people are being surrounded by a wealth of good nutrition information. Yet old ingrained habits and ways of looking at things often die hard.

Similarly, reformation in the evangelical church is going to require some massive paradigm shifts in the way we think. The pop evangelical church world, in many ways, is analogous to the world of fast-food chains. New tastes will need to be acquired and cultivated if we are going to experience an appreciation for the riches of the reformation in the church. Moreover, there are a few hurdles that we must get over, and about which we ought to be much in prayer, if we are to see any progress in reforming evangelicalism in the near future.

We have previously touched upon some of these hurdles. Sometimes a person may have been in an environment with some sort of great Reformational or evangelical label attached to it, which, in reality, was something quite different—and quite bad. This can take many forms. Often churches with an evangelical or Reformed label are filled with legalism and/or emotional detachment. Consequently those labels for some may have left a repugnant taste for any and all things evangelical and/or Reformational.

Similarly, the hurdle can involve guilt by another kind of association. Very often people grow up with a formal liturgy emptied of the power of the gospel. There are many evangelicals, having come from Liberal Protestant or Roman Catholic backgrounds, who testify to this phenomena. As a result, the great beautiful historic liturgical forms for conveying the gift of the gospel have become repugnant to them. College parachurch ministries for recent generations may have unwittingly contributed to this problem to some extent. It is at the university level where many young people raised in empty religious formalism with an emphasis on works righteousness do become exposed to the glorious truths of the gospel. However, the worship environments in such settings are almost always very informal. The "reformation" in the lives of these young people therefore ends up corresponding more to the historic radical reformation of the enthusiasts than to the reformation itself. The irony is that the InterVarsity Christian Fellowship movement, for instance, was largely driven by leaders such as more formal Anglican authors John Stott and J. I. Packer and Presbyterian authors James Montgomery Boice and Francis Schaefer. The evangelical generations influenced by their writings would probably be shocked by their style and practice of more formal liturgical worship. They would likely expect that these leaders, like themselves, essentially would have been sitting in a circle singing "*Kumbaya.*" They would find it unimaginable that formal liturgical worship is what fueled their evangelistic zeal and resulting work. It is very important to remember that the differences evangelicals have with Roman Catholicism, for instance, are primarily doctrinal. While there are certainly differences in worship, the primary difference certainly ought not to be viewed as a matter of pop culture vs. high culture!

Sometimes people grow up in a particularly good Reformational denominational church setting as unbelievers, are actually converted in a different church setting and cannot appreciate that their original church setting was never the problem as much as their own heart was. You can, therefore, have vastly different recollections among those who grew up in the very same church. Some recall their experience as sheer boredom and enduring church services counting the organ pipes. Others recall hymns, catechism teachings and former preachers with great fondness. Those with the bad memories will often land in a different denomination with a different theology simply as a reaction to the feelings they experienced and having come alive and "seen the light" in a different setting.

Sometimes "new persuasive words for degraded or defaced ones" can be helpful.[1] It is indeed a challenge to write about reformation, restoring liturgical elements and unearthing the treasures of old when sins have been committed in the name of Reformation and liturgy and/or when someone just doesn't appreciate them as a result of a prior negative experience. It is a challenge to expect true reformation to emanate from denominations which have cultural and historical baggage attached to them. New words and new churches can help. Ultimately, however, as truth never changes and as God's power is in his word, there are words that can and need to be reclaimed. There can be healing. A person previously abused by a father may have difficulty celebrating the fatherhood of God. In fact, they will probably be powerfully motivated to call God something else. Healing will happen when we get straight in our minds which is the analogy and which is the standard. "It's not God who is an analogy of human fatherhood; it's human fatherhood that is either a good or bad analogy of [God's fatherhood]."[2] Likewise, with the biblical riches of the Reformation, we need to begin judging the analogy by the standard, not the other way around.

Finally, another big hurdle is hypocrisy. Hypocrisy, of course, is everywhere, including Reformational churches. To one extent or another we are all hypocrites. There is, though, a perception among some that unregenerate, total phonies have an easier time of hiding behind their masks in these churches as opposed to pop evangelical churches. And there may be a degree of truth to that! In fact, this has been a driving factor in Wesleyan holiness and subsequent Pentecostal movements. On the other hand, while legalistic holiness environments seem to produce godly, upright behavior outwardly, it actually produces far more scandalous behavior in the end.

What many don't realize is that a certain tolerance or grace toward the suspected hypocrite is intentional in Reformational churches, having to do with how Reformational churches define themselves in light of Scripture. Based on Scripture, the church is defined as both people and place.[3] It is both an organism and an institution. As to place, it is not a building *per se*, but it is the place where the word is rightly preached and the sacraments faithfully administered, with some degree of order/discipline. The people

---

1. Zahl, "New Persuasive Words."
2. Horton commenting on Lloyd Jones, "Lord's Prayer (Part 1)."
3. Horton, *People and Place*.

or membership of the church is based upon a credible profession of faith in Jesus Christ as Lord and Savior by the individual who has and continues to repent of his sins (meaning a change of mind whereby he agrees with Jesus that such things are wrong and thus he ultimately disdains the sins to which he is prone). Unlike many pop evangelical churches, it is not based upon requiring a further personal testimony to a subjective born again "experience" and an observable changed life to see if you really, really, really believe.

Reformational churches believe that such attempted readings of the heart cross the line that Jesus drew for us. *It is not for us to try to figure out who is truly regenerate.* Jesus commanded that we not try to separate the weeds from the wheat. He very specifically warned against doing so: "But he said, 'No, lest in gathering the weeds you root up the wheat along with them. Let both grow together until the harvest, and at harvest time I will tell the reapers, Gather the weeds first and bind them in bundles to be burned, but gather the wheat into my barn'" (Matt 13:29–30). Similarly, we ought to be emulating his pastoral care: "a bruised reed he will not break, and a smoldering wick he will not quench, until he brings justice to victory" (Matt 12:20; Isa 42:3). Therefore, Reformational churches recognize that the visible church consists of a mixed body. The ultimate "real" invisible church is known to Christ and it is ultimately up to him to do the separating.

Nor are there two tiers of Christians with some being first class "spiritual" due to a supposed "second blessing" and others just second-class "carnal" Christians. This Wesleyan and Pentecostal idea is foreign to Scripture. There is one track for all believers, not two. To be sure, some are further along the track in maturity than others. As a result, not only is there the one who may seem like an out and out fake to deal with, but there is often simply the weaker brother or sister who needs our loving patience. Now, if a member of the church is living in open, scandalous unrepentant sin, there certainly is discipline lovingly designed to restore that person. Moreover, we are called to holiness; but to judge the heart based upon a subjective experience or our perception of a transformed life is simply not part of the biblical criteria for membership in the visible church. Moreover, trying to motivate holiness by creating our own categories of super Christian and nominal Christian is simply not part of the Reformation (or biblical) equation. As to suspected hypocrites, we are to "suck it up" and concern ourselves with the beam in our own eye (Matt 7:3–5). As to the bruised

Part 3: Some Additional Liberating Applications and Implications

reeds and smoldering wicks, we are to cherish and nurture them, rather than break them or snuff them out.

24

His Utmost for My Highest

WHEN LAW AND GOSPEL become confused or when law becomes over emphasized, zeal can become a dangerous thing. One of the books considered a devotional classic by many pop evangelicals is Oswald Chambers' *My Utmost for His Highest*. There is no question that this book contains many wonderful reflections of Scripture and the spurring on of its readers to good deeds, yet many commentators have observed that there are serious problems with this work, particularly when it comes to legalism and mysticism. The title itself would seem to fly in the face of Scripture. It is very much like when we turn the Divine Service on its head and make it about us and very much like when we gravitate to the law over the gospel. *The Bible is, after all, the story about his utmost for my highest, not the other way around.*

To draw from both Rod Rosenbladt and a Mike Myers' movie character, sometimes we put the wrong "em-PHA-sis" on a particular "syl-LA-ble."[1] Doing this in our lives can sometimes lead to very unintended and serious consequences. Many examples could be cited where pop evangelicals have exhibited a misguided zeal, sometimes dangerous to others and even to their own detriment. Oswald Chambers himself zealously volunteered to assist the YMCA in Egypt during WWI, where he died at age forty-three. He didn't die, though, as a result of war related injury. He died from complications following an appendectomy after he zealously continued to work with appendicitis without timely stopping to get the medical

---

1. Rosenbladt, "Creed or Chaos?"; and see *View from the Top*, quoted by the character John Whitney, http://www.imdb.com/title/tt0264150/quotes.

PART 3: SOME ADDITIONAL LIBERATING APPLICATIONS AND IMPLICATIONS

attention he needed. Evangelicals, particularly those with type-A personalities, sometimes need to be warned against throwing caution to the wind in their unbridled zeal. In our railings against spiritual lethargy, which we tend to think type B's are more prone to, we miss the danger on the other side of the spectrum. The ends never justify the means and there have been times when common sense gets thrown out in the name of the mission. I recall listening to a mission trip team leader report on a trip they had just returned from. The leaders had ignorantly put the team of teenagers up in a very dangerous inner city area and consequently found themselves in a situation where their safety was compromised. He went on to compare himself and this "hardship" to the Apostle Paul and his hardships. The problem is that I don't ever recall Paul pitching his tent in a bad area, much less ever being "persecuted" for exercising poor judgment, which is something we are all prone to do.

In 2003 David Bloom, an NBC correspondent, was assigned to cover the Iraq war. He traveled day and night on the advancing front line with a military convoy. Bloom, a Roman Catholic, had recently been attending an interdenominational Bible study and felt bolstered by a newfound excitement for faith and life. Spending long days and nights in the cramped quarters in the bottom of a tank, he began to suffer leg cramps. Ignoring the advice to seek medical attention, he zealously plodded on. Due to a pulmonary embolism which developed, he suddenly dropped dead at the age of thirty-nine. In his last email to his wife, he told her that he had moved Oswald Chambers' book *My Utmost for His Highest*, which was a devotional of the Bible study, to his breast pocket as he wanted to keep it close to his heart.[2]

Like Chambers' death, Bloom's death was not necessary. Both were zealously serving in wartime in the Middle East, but neither died from war-related injuries. Both suffered primarily due to their consuming passion. We need to caution ourselves to maintain a proper balance. Christ's passion was all consuming so that mine need not be. He sacrificed his life, so that I need not. He sold everything he had and gave to the poor, so I need not impoverish myself. His yoke is easy and his burden is light. The sacrifices he desires from us are a broken spirit and a contrite heart. Sometimes sacrifice of life at the hands of others is inevitable and out of our control; however, we ought not to needlessly sacrifice our lives by our own neglect in the name of mission, whatever that mission might be. Having said that, as we

2. See Metaxas, "But Sweet Will Be the Flower."

observed earlier, we all leave mixed legacies. While both men's lives appropriately continue to serve as fascinating inspirations for many, no one leaves a perfect legacy when it comes to our actions. Christ died for that too. It is Christ's legacy that ultimately matters. Those who profess union with him, like Chambers and Bloom, are honored as heroes of the faith precisely because they are found in him, despite whatever personal shortcomings we all might exhibit from time to time. Noted author and personal friend of Bloom, Eric Metaxas, gives a moving eulogy of Bloom, recounting God's amazing sovereignty at work in the circumstances surrounding his death.[3]

In the past many Christians exhibited a misguided zeal when it came to evangelism. Their life came to be defined by their evangelizing, even if it was done on company time. They didn't understand that we are citizens of two kingdoms. They failed to observe the cultural commission and great commandment given to them by God in their vocations as individual members of the civil kingdom. Furthermore, as citizens of the heavenly kingdom, they misread the great commission as a direct and immediate responsibility of the individual. In fact, the great commission was given to the apostles and, consequently, to the church as an institution. As members of that institution we participate in this commission by supporting the local church, foreign missionaries and appropriately (even zealously) bearing witness to our hope in our everyday lives. We need not burden ourselves directly and immediately as individuals with the whole responsibility of going to the ends of the earth preaching and baptizing. Our responsibility is indirect and mediated. Even those specially called as missionaries go as sent representatives of the church, not as individuals. Moreover, since it is God who has established our dual citizenship, one cannot properly fulfill their responsibility as a citizen of the heavenly kingdom without fulfilling their responsibility as a citizen of the civil kingdom as well.

---

3. See ibid.

25

A Radical Me or a Radical Grace?

ALONG THE SAME LINES are the contemporary buzzwords "personal transformation," and the call to be a "radical" or "fully devoted" or "sold out" Christian, though the emphasis has shifted, more or less, from personal evangelism to social justice. These exhortations now have been ramped up significantly by a younger, more globally connected, more socially conscious generation. These more contemporary exhortations often result from a confusion of categories. There has been a profound change in social consciousness and our ability to connect with everyone around the world. The Internet and social media have produced a radical change in the world and in that sense it is appropriate to encourage Christians of their need to get radical or be radical in light of all of the new opportunities presented by technology. The Internet has radically turned the world into a virtual village. There are, though, some significant dangers in this. One, we can lose sight of the ordinary opportunities in life and everything becomes programmatic, much like small groups can in our interpersonal relationships. Two, we can quickly fall into another performance quagmire, especially when we confuse categories and radical is used to describe faith itself, rather than merely the new changes in opportunity offered by social media.

Here again the focus quickly shifts from Christ to the Christian. The fact of the matter is that in this age there was, is, and ever will be, just one who was radical, fully devoted and sold out and his name is Jesus. Despite the fact that a number of contemporary churches now appear to get the fact that sanctification is gospel-driven rather than me-driven, they still try to verify, measure and keep score by looking at one's transformation. This is simply a contemporary version of the third use of the law gobbling up the first use and the ongoing use of the gospel that we alluded to earlier. It just results in a new legalism. Now, it's about playing the same old game with new rules and a new scoring system. Spirituality continues to be equated with busyness and with being social. Specifically, we continue to measure spirituality by how busy and social one is with church-related activities; however, today it's not about Bible studies, choir practice and campaigning for moral causes. Today in many evangelical churches it's all about small group attendance, how many "mission" trips one goes on and how often one helps the poor. To make sure one gets credit for these good deeds, many literally wear them on their sleeves. Besides the customized T-shirt from the latest mission trip, there's the Facebook montage of pictures and, of course, the music video produced for everyone in church to see. But wait a minute, doesn't Scripture say not to give to the needy to be seen by others and that even our left hand shouldn't know what our right hand is doing? (Matt 6:3).

To take our eyes off of Jesus and put them on ourselves and our transformation for our own assurance concerning our faith, i.e., to justify ourselves before God is an endless, ugly quagmire. One popular author has said we should all be giving up a week a year to serve the poor. Clearly, such an exhortation is not one which is set forth in Scripture. This type of exhorting can take away a Christian's sense of freedom, binding his or her conscience. People being made to feel like deer caught in the headlights, unless they have a portfolio of "mission" trips to offer up, along with some self-made music videos as evidence, is now far too common in evangelicalism. This can become a sort of spiritual terrorism or bullying where people are consequently made to feel like they are "unspiritual" second class Christians. Pastors can easily foster this sort of thing by falling prey to their own egos. They can easily seek to exalt their church's ministries which promote their "vision" by loading them on the backs of those who already have a full plate serving God and bearing witness in their own vocations. *There can be a thin line between legitimately encouraging people to better bear witness to the love of Christ in their vocations and using people as pawns in building one's own ministry or kingdom.*

We need to return to the biblical teaching of quietly serving one's neighbor through our multiple vocations, without the introspection of constantly congratulating ourselves or of beating ourselves up. Allow me to

Part 3: Some Additional Liberating Applications and Implications

illustrate here with some personal examples. As I look back on some of my different vocations in which I had served throughout my life, I can now see that there are many ways of helping the poor that just happened in the ordinary course of living. For a number of years I had served as a deacon in my church. Every Monday evening the deacons would meet to literally count the money from the church offerings, confidentially and anonymously log in contributions for individuals' IRS reporting, and have meetings to distribute the extra monies collected for benevolence aside from the church's budget and mission funds. We would address and administer the requests for assistance from both within the immediate congregation as well as from surrounding sister congregations. As another example, for about ten years I had the opportunity as a lawyer to serve as a part-time public defender in an urban area. For a small stipend from the municipality, I spent one evening a month, from six o'clock in the evening to about one o'clock in the morning, representing a long line of impoverished people who were charged with various offenses and who could not afford to hire an attorney. Now, here's the danger, even in the ordinary things, if we're not careful. Even by today's new evangelical "radical" standards, I'm now feeling pretty good about myself since just my second example comes to about two work weeks per year when I add up the hours! But taking our eyes off of Jesus and putting them on ourselves is never a good idea. I'm then plagued by the thought that God just doesn't look at the outward acts but also demands perfect motivation. I know my motives are never pure. As a matter of fact, to any extent that I was trying to score points with God, they were pretty damningly selfish. Additionally, I could have done so much more. My introspection brings me up and then back down again.

Therefore, in an effort to again redeem myself and bring myself back up, I naturally look for another good example. I begin to think about how my social consciousness has improved over the years. We are routinely programmatic when it comes to relief or missions work. In our very compartmentalized lives, while we might go anywhere on a missions or relief trip, we will amazingly avoid poor countries like the plague when it comes to our vacations, even though they really need our commerce. When I went to the Caribbean, I didn't go to the rich, safer places, but happened to be on a cruise that stopped in more dangerous areas, poor countries like Haiti and Jamaica. I made sure that I spent a few dollars to help out the locals there in their vocations—something they desperately needed. Now I'm feeling pretty good again until I'm reminded that I'm starting to puff up like an

A Radical Me or a Radical Grace?

inflatable character in Macy's Thanksgiving Day parade. Then I'm again convicted of sin and realize that I should have done so much more and so much better shared the reason for my hope with people along the way. That would have turned the trip into a true "mission" trip of sorts as well.

And I could go on. Once we start down this road of introspection, I would want you to know about all my other giving of time, talent and treasure. And it would get uglier. To appease my own conscience, I would want to remind those who are obsessed with helping the poor, that there are many more things we are called to do in life besides just serving the poor. I would want to cross examine those who have obsessed with humanitarian relief mission trips—did they not sacrifice some of their other callings, such as being an attentive spouse, a loving parent or a diligent employee? In fact, did they not sometimes end up ultimately sacrificing others in their quest to get what they think will be a seat of honor in heaven, rather than truly sacrificing themselves for those God has placed in their care? The point is that there is an endless vacillating between pharisaism and despair when we take our eyes off of Jesus and start to look within.

A primary point of the story of the rich young ruler is that we cannot save ourselves or the world. We simply cannot pull it off from down here. The law is too demanding and the world is too fallen. We do have one who did pull it off. As Tullian Tchividjian has observed, God requires "Christ's perfection, not our progress."[1] Only in Christ do we have that perfection in which to rest. It is impossible to rest in our flawed personal transformation. When we do that, we start to sound like those Jesus rebukes, who on the last day say, Lord, have I not done? Have I not done? Have I not done? (Matt 7:22). His implicit answer is: no you have not! But to his own he says it is done: "It is finished" (John 19:30). It is for freedom that he has set us free. As the Heidelberg Disputation puts it, "The law says do and it is never done. Grace says believe in this and everything is already done."[2] The gospel says done. We all need to learn to live in light of that. Doing enough for the poor can never be done which is precisely why we need a Savior! *Jesus was the only rich young ruler who could earn eternal life by giving it all away without leaving himself impoverished. He is not asking us to do that anymore than he was asking Abraham to follow through and really sacrifice his son! He graciously took care of both for us. Similarly, Jesus was the Good Samaritan who crossed the road from heaven to earth for us who were lying on the side*

---

1. Tchividjian, *One Way Love*, 98.
2. 1518 Heidelberg Disputation, thesis 26.

PART 3: SOME ADDITIONAL LIBERATING APPLICATIONS AND IMPLICATIONS

of the road. One of Jesus' points is that it would have been impossible for the priest and the Levite to fulfill their God given functions in Jerusalem had they defiled themselves with the blood of the victim. It is Jesus who could and did bind our wounds, nourish us with the wine of communion and give us sanctuary in the church until he returns.[3] Again we see that the Scriptures are all about him and his fulfilling of the law, not us and our attempts to do so.

Out of gratitude for what Christ has accomplished for us, we ought to share the reason for the hope that we have with others, invite them to church and have compassion on the poor in the ordinary activities of life. *Then life itself will become a mission trip and a humanitarian relief trip, even as we also serve others through our vocations.* If we keep our eyes fixed on Jesus, the trip through life will be much more joyful as well. And, as Gomer Pyle would say: "Surprise, surprise, surprise," we are transformed as the work he began in us is brought to completion. (If you're not old enough to have watched Gomer Pyle, you can check him out on YouTube.)

---

3. See Fisk, "Glawspel Redux."

26

Knowing and Doing God's Will in My Life

While most Christians struggle with the issue of knowing and doing God's will to some degree, I never realized the amount of consternation this subject has caused for so many Christians. When we pray, "Thy will be done," or, "Father, help us to do your will," the Father intends this to provide a sense of comfort for his children. Instead, what we find is that there is often endless worry and neurotic speculation among many evangelicals as to what God's will is for them in any given situation and whether they are walking in it. And so when it comes to picking a college, a career, a spouse and so forth, there are often pervasive clouds of doubt and anxiety overhead. To exacerbate the situation, many then look for signs or to circumstances of success or failure as barometers to measure if they are doing God's will. When things go bad, they conclude that they must be outside of God's will. When things go well, they reason that they must be walking within God's will and are under his protective umbrella. The end result is once again either guilt and despair or selfish pride. Either I'm outside of God's will and being punished for it or I've managed to divine God's will through my devotional diligence and am being blessed as a result. Like Roman Catholicism would teach, I have therefore earned his favor.

The problem is that many contemporary evangelicals do not understand that God has a revealed will and a secret will and that it is only his revealed will with which we are to be concerned with figuring out. He has laid out his perfect will in Scripture which is sufficient for all of life. Where he has spoken, we ought to follow what he says. Where he is silent, we are given this wonderful gift called Christian freedom to make choices. The choices made within this realm of Christian freedom are, in fact, a part God's secret will in which he uses the choices we make to work all things out for our good. It is one of the wonderful gifts he gives to his children, the gift of freedom along with the promise that he will bless, guide and work it all out for my good with his fatherly hand. Therefore, through the study of his word and prayer, we can increasingly better understand his revealed will as to what is right and wrong. When our choices are among equally moral alternatives for which the Bible gives little or no guidance, i.e., his secret will, we should not look for a "sign" or a special revelation from God. We are free to simply pray for guidance and use the faculties God has given us. By gathering information, seeking the wisdom of others, weighing opportunities, assessing our qualifications and the needs of our neighbors, we can rest in the knowledge of his providential care as we make our life's decisions.[1]

This was another area where the Reformation again got it right. Among the *solas* of the Reformation discussed earlier is the doctrine of *sola Scriptura*, i.e., Scripture alone. There is nothing in the Bible which would suggest that Jesus is like a sphinx and that it is our job to try to unlock the riddles of the universe. God's will is not a code for us to break with the assistance of private revelation. This is a purely pagan notion that has corrupted and polluted the thinking on this subject in much of the contemporary evangelical world. Such thinking arises from something the Reformers called enthusiasm, which is a sibling to mysticism, gnosticism and sentimentalism. Enthusiasm is the notion that God, by the Holy Spirit, speaks in a direct immediate way to me, rather than through his mediated Word, the Bible. The Reformation properly understood that when the pope in Rome purported to pronounce a new word from God, such a word was not on a par with Scripture. More than that, they also properly understood that the radical enthusiasts, who were on the other end of the spectrum claiming direct unmediated revelations from God, were nothing more than each person attempting to be a pope unto him or herself. Over the years there have been many evangelical leaders with such a visionary mindset who have sought to bind the consciences of their followers by making pronouncements, i.e., pontificating, on things where Scripture is silent. Indeed, "vision casting" by "vision casting leaders" has become all the rage in the

---

1. See Palmer, *Holy Spirit*, 129–131.

church marketing movement. Evangelicals need to once again be serious about listening to God only where he has spoken, through Scripture alone.

Doing God's will cannot be measured by our perceived success or failure. According to Scripture, faithfulness, not success, is what we are called to. As a matter of fact, we are pretty much promised that faithfulness will bring persecution and suffering rather than accolades of popularity. Suffering in such circumstances does not mean God's disfavor. According to Scripture it is a privilege for the believer to share in Christ's suffering. *Like nothing else, persecution has a way of vividly demonstrating the hatred and utter moral bankruptcy of the persecutors and, at the same time, the love of the persecuted and the priceless moral value of what they die for—Christ and his work.* It has often been said that the blood of the martyrs is the seed of the church. To be clear, in Christianity, the martyr is never the killer, but rather is the innocent one killed by another for his or her loving witness concerning Christ.

27

The Practical Relational Implications (Less Arguing, Less Frustration)

UNDERSTANDING THAT THE PERFECT active obedience of Christ has already been imputed to the Christian has enormous practical and relational implications. First, as we have seen, it frees us from the illusion of thinking we can achieve perfection in this life. We no longer need vacillate between self-righteousness and despair. We are freed from the tyranny of our own identity and find our true identity in being hidden in Christ. We need not psychologically go through life as a sentimentalist, with rose colored glasses, trying to focus on my glass being half full instead of half empty. I am free to acknowledge that my glass will never be full this side of heaven. While I continue to strive, I am not burdened. His yoke is easy and his burden is light (Matt 11: 28–30). But there is more.

Despite his shortcomings (and perhaps because of them) Tullian Tchividjian has done a lot to bring home the practical and psychological benefits of these biblical teachings in a contemporary pastoral context. He writes that because of this imputed perfect obedience of Jesus, we stand before the Father having total approval, affection, acceptance, love, security, freedom, worth, among other things, for all eternity.[1] As a result, *there is tremendous liberation in knowing that we ultimately do not need to obtain these things from others.* Therefore, not only am I free from myself, but I am also free from imposing unrealistic expectations on others to meet my needs. Since I have everything I need in Christ already, I don't need to put

---

1. See Tchividjian, *Jesus + Nothing = Everything*, 77, 92, 205–6.

The Practical Relational Implications

a burden on others as a result of my need to receive affirmation, validation, etc. from them. I am free to also accept them as glasses that will never be full this side of eternity. Freed from over realized expectations in our personal relationships in this present age, we can increasingly appreciate and enjoy catching glimpses and bits of transformation by grace in ourselves and others along the imperfect way. These glimpses and pieces simply point us forward to the age to come when all will be made perfect and glorified.

This simple truth can revolutionize our relationships. If I am a spouse, I am not only reckoned to be a perfect spouse before the Father through Christ, I also have the perfect spouse in Christ. Consequently, besides finding my own righteous identity in Christ and not in me, I can also accept my imperfect spouse because I also already have a perfect spouse in Christ. While he could have run off with the devil and avoided the cross, he chose to be faithful and went to hell and back to rescue me. One day that marriage will be fully and perfectly consummated for all eternity. Since I have everything I need in Christ, ultimately, I do not need my spouse to meet my every need for affirmation, approval, affection, validation, etc. These things are nice and enjoyable to be sure, and, as foretastes, also point us forward to that day when it will all be perfect. However, as Tchividjian has observed, I don't need them in the sense that "I no longer require [them] from anyone else."[2] I no longer need to be emotionally needy. In an ultimate sense, I can give and love liberally without needing anything in return. I am a spouse who already has it all. Similarly, if I am a child, since I already have a perfect parent in God the Father, I don't need my parents to be perfect. I have been adopted as a child of the trillionaire king of the universe. I have everything to give and no need to get. Again, if I am a parent, I have the perfect child in Christ who loves me unconditionally. If I am a sibling, I have the perfect elder brother in Christ who sacrifices for my needs. I am therefore free to accept my own children and siblings without tyrannizing or manipulating them in order to have my emotional needs met. *The gospel can make our relationships thrive in a way that our mere innate sense of obligation never can.*

This does not mean that there should be no receiving in our various relationships. Carried too far, one might be tempted to conclude that there should be no give and take in a given relationship. We must remember that from the beginning, God, in his providence, specifically provides for these relationships (vocations) so that we can provide for one another's actual, real and legitimate needs in this world. What this realization of the Father's

---

2 Ibid., 92.

acceptance does do is to help fill in all of the many gaps where sin has fractured these earthly relationships. It helps us begin to restore those relationships which will one day be made perfect where there will be perfect giving and receiving.

All of this is to say that we are liberated, not only from ourselves, but that we are also free to truly love others unconditionally. *On account of Christ, I can give myself "dearly loved of God" as an extra middle name. Since I have all I need in Christ, I can also interpose the words "I'm freed to love" in front of everyone else's name in the world, whether friend or foe.* Moreover, these thoughts are not based upon some nice fairy tale to make us feel better about ourselves. There are some very real psychological, practical and relational implications, but they are not based on just another flimsy self-esteem house of cards. They are grounded in the truth of the Christian faith which is firmly grounded in history. The implications, therefore, are all the stronger because these things are real and not merely psychological crutches or opiates of some sort.

28

Our Heavenly Inheritance

OUR PILGRIMAGE ON THIS earth certainly has its hardships. Throughout the Scriptures believers are encouraged and consoled by God's promises concerning our heavenly inheritance or heavenly reward ("which is always singular in the NT"[1]—e.g., Col 3:24; 1 Pet 1:3–4). It refers to the glorious eternal life which awaits us when we will be like him because we shall see him as he is (1 John 3:2) and will behold his face (Rev 22:4). There are several references to believers receiving a crown (1 Cor 9:25; 1 Thess 2:19; 2 Tim 4:8; Jas 1:12; 1 Pet 5:4). Jesus himself is our reward (Phil 3:8). Our heavenly Father promises us that we will inherit the whole earth (Matt 5:5; Rev 5). We are assured that our present sufferings are not worth comparing to the glory that will be revealed (Rom 8:18). We are told to "rejoice and be glad, for your reward is great in heaven" (Matt 5:12). The bliss that awaits us is described as "fullness of joy; at your right hand are pleasures forevermore" (Ps 16:11).

It's almost embarrassingly scandalous that God would refer to any of our inheritance as a reward. After all, he is the one doing all of the earning and meriting. He not only fulfilled all righteousness for our justification but he continues the good work he began in us as he sanctifies and glorifies us. A branch not grafted to the vine can do nothing (John 15:4–5). Good works before a holy God are impossible without the superimposing of Christ's work upon ours. In justifying us he makes us coheirs and unites

---

[1] Justin Taylor, on John Starke's "You Asked," July 18, 2011, http://www.thegospelcoalition.org/article/you-asked-what-are-the-rewards-in-heaven-jesus-talks-about.

us to himself giving us the privilege already in this life of beginning to participate in yielding the fruit of good works. As the Heidelberg Catechism puts it at Q. 114: "In this life even the holiest have only a small beginning of the [new] obedience (Eccl 7:20; Rom 7:14; 1 John 1:8–10)." To try to put this in perspective, imagine for a moment a billionaire father who has ransomed some young children out of extreme poverty and slavery. He then adopts them as his own, making them heirs of his estate, with which he is intimately involved in taking care of. It's kind of like this father mowing the lawn and delighting in letting his young children take turns to "help" push the mower as the father does the real work and then rewards the children for the work accomplished. That's how gracious our Heavenly Father is in all of this!

Rather than bask in this childlike faith, we tend to be like the mother of James and John when she asked for special seats of honor for her sons. We take ourselves a little too seriously and do not take seriously enough our utter dependence upon Jesus. There seem to be two prevalent errors concerning this subject by which we are constantly prone to jump the biblical tracks: first, thinking that we are earning our reward and, second, ascribing a negative or punishing aspect to heaven if we acknowledge even the possibility of variation of reward among individuals.

The first common error is that we begin to think that we are earning or meriting the reward that Christ earned for us. The central teaching which the Reformers sought to correct was Rome's doctrine of justification. Rome had taught justification before God was a cooperative effort whereby we merit the merit of Christ through our good works. The Reformers believed that this was a mistake, due in part, to an error in the Latin Vulgate version of the Bible. "Obviously, being *made* righteous is quite a different thing than from being *declared* righteous. By itself, the latter term does not require the evangelical doctrine of justification, but it does render erroneous the Vulgate's translation and therefore the interpretation of justification as moral transformation."[2] Since the Reformation, many pop evangelicals as well as Reformational evangelicals, sometimes while even ostensibly holding to the doctrine of an imputed active obedience from God, have, nonetheless, let works righteousness in through the back door. Many believe that grace gets you into heaven, but that we are earning or meriting rewards for when we get there. They might move "purgatory" inside of heaven, as it were,

---

2. Taken from *The Christian Faith*, by Michael Horton, 631 (copyright © [2011 by Michael Horton]), use by permission of Zondervan, www.zondervan.com.

but they become functionally Roman Catholic in their thinking. We have previously touched on a related issue in chapter 23 above where we noted the spiritual/carnal dichotomy held by many pop evangelicals.

That our promised heavenly reward is not based upon our merit is one of the most difficult subjects to wrap our sinful brains around. This is partly because two things are going on at the same time when it comes to righteousness or good works: law and gospel. It is law insofar as law is being fulfilled on account of Christ's work on our behalf which yields rewards; it is gospel grace that we are receiving. Christ's gift of righteousness is imputed to me as through a vine to its branch, not only for my justification, but also for my sanctification and ultimate glorification as well. These are gifts of grace I receive as I am grafted into Christ. He is bringing to completion the good work he began in me. Christ's work continues in and through me and I share in bearing fruit not because of my merit but because of his grace. Therefore, our reward is not earned or merited by us. It is not in the nature of a wage, bonus or a pension for our faithful service. For us, it is in the nature of a wild and crazy inheritance which has been earned/merited by Christ for his faithful service. He graciously shares this with and in those who have been adopted as his brothers and sisters who have been grafted into his body.

Our reward is a word of gospel grace that we by nature are prone to turn back into law for ourselves to fulfill. The general law throughout Scripture that judgment will be according to works is exactly that—law. As we have seen, the gospel is graciously given because, Adam, Israel and we could not and cannot fulfill the requirements of the law. Therefore, God graciously takes on human form in Jesus Christ to fulfill the law on our behalf (Matt 5:17). Romans 3 makes it clear that no one except Christ has satisfied the law, i.e., the covenant of works which he reiterated in ch. 2. By virtue of our union with Christ, we share in the inheritance he earned as branches on a vine. He is our reward. Heaven is our reward. The inheritance has been laid up for us (Col 1:5). There is nothing we can merit or demerit or add or subtract concerning our justification, sanctification and glorification before God. My justification is done and finished on account of everything Christ did and now imputes to me. My sanctification and glorification are being actively accomplished through the good works that he works through me subsequent to my justification. Again, a branch by itself can do nothing. My best works are as filthy rags before a holy God and can only be counted as righteous on account of Christ. It is, therefore, our faith that is rewarded, on account of Christ, not our works.[3] The Reformers carefully postulated that our judgment is according to works, not on the basis of them. Calvin quotes Augustine: "Faithful is the Lord, who hath made himself our debtor, not by receiving anything from us, but by promising us all things."[4] He further states: "Let it be a fixed principle in our hearts that the kingdom of heaven is not the hire of servants, but the inheritance of sons (Eph 1:18)."[5] The reward is based on his promise not our merit.[6] We are to labor, not for our own profit, but "for the glory of God."[7] "God rewards good works, but it is through his grace that He crowns his gifts."[8]

Professor Linebaugh writes:

> The standard reformational way to talk about the relationship between justification and judgment takes its cue from Paul's prepositions: justification is through/by (διά/ἐκ) faith and judgment is according to (κατά + accusative) works. This pattern of speech makes a theological point: the basis or ground of our justification is Jesus Christ, the righteous one, who is received through/by faith; the evidence or testimony of God's love evoking love is the fruit produced by the Holy Spirit. This means that whereas justification (i.e., God's final judgment verdict, announced in the present) is based on Jesus' righteousness given in the word and received through faith, the judgment referred to in passages like Romans 14:10–12 and 2 Corinthians 5:10 will *correspond* to the fruits of faith produced by the Spirit—and this because "he who began a good work in you will bring it to completion at the day of Jesus Christ (Phil 1:6)."[9]

Therefore, to those who place their faith in him, he crowns his good works which he works in and through us. He makes clean our best efforts which are as filthy rags. On account of Christ's mediation, the Father can delight in the works accomplished in and through us.

My motive becomes mercenary when I think that I will merit honor before God or even honor along with God by everyone else for my groveling

---

3. See Wilken, "Listener Email and the Issues, Etc. Comment Line, 5/3/13."

4. Calvin, *Institutes*, bk. III, ch. XVIII, sect. 7, p. 126.

5. Ibid., 120.

6. *Triglot Concordia*, Defense of the Augsburg Confession, "Of Love and Fulfilling the Law," art. V, no. 241, http://bookofconcord.org/defense_5_love.php.

7. Ibid., art. V, no. 243.

8. Belgic Confession of Faith, art. XXIV, in *Psalter Hymnal*, p. 69.

9. Tchvidjian, quoting Linebaugh, "Good News of Final Judgement."

service. Such a motivated work produces no crown of reward. Believing that we are earning or even facilitating rewards for ourselves is an insidious form of greed and ambition. It is the ultimate self-love. It completely lacks a fundamental element of what a good work is. It is the very opposite of what our justification frees us to be: a people loving others to the glory of God proceeding from faith in Christ. This is faith working through love (Gal 5:6). The minute I start thinking in terms of my merit, my motives have gone south, disqualifying my works from being good works at all. It is precisely those works which need the most filtering by Christ to count for anything! In fact, such thinking (like a lazy and ambivalent attitude on the other end of the spectrum) might just signal that a branch is not connected to the vine at all! As we previously observed, it is to those who rely on their works, saying, "Lord, have I not done? Lord, have I not done?" that he will say, "I never knew you" (Matt 7:22–23). It is here that many ministers, even well-known and respected ones, seem to sometimes fall into a smug trap of thinking that the performing of their sacred vocation gives them an inside track for a life well lived and worthy of special honor. Pastor Curtis is well worth quoting at length regarding this point:

> If those who work only one hour receive the same pay as those who have borne the heat of the day—why bother? If good works cannot save, shall we go on sinning that grace may abound?
>
> This is why only the gospel, the real gospel of grace alone and unconditional election (which are the same thing), can motivate good works. It is the only thing that can cut through the mercenary instinct in the fallen human mind. Is saving our skins the only possible motivation for good works? What a narrow and odd doctrine. God had to kill it with the gospel. Is the desire to lord it over another and be a little god who can save some and damn others by action or inaction the only possible motivation for preaching the gospel and giving to the church? What a bizarre notion. God had to kill it with the doctrine of election.
>
> For consider what happens to Christian freedom and that hearty Lutheran [Christian] joy in God's creation under the Functional Arminian scheme. What is more important: your child's college education or the saving of souls? How can you spend all that money that could have gone to missions? How dare you have a hobby that takes time that could have been spent in door to door evangelism! For surely, a soul saved is more important that a fishing trip. How can you in good conscience plunk down hundreds of dollars for a family vacation when that money could have been

used to save a soul? Those who take this doctrine seriously are already raffling off cars at Easter Sunday services. I salute them for having the courage of their convictions. If we can save people with our actions, if we must do whatever we can to get people into the church to hear the Word because God works through means—then woe to us if we don't give a car away every week to get folks to show up, or flat out pay unbelievers to show up to hear the Word—woe to us if we spend even one dime on a cruise to Cozumel rather than on a missionary's ticket to some Godforsaken land.

But that is the road back to monasticism—the height of the peculiarly Roman version of this doctrine. The best thing you can do is dedicate your whole life, lock, stock, and barrel to the saving of souls. Everything else is second best, selfish, and carnal.

But Luther overthrew all those notions with the gospel of grace alone—that is, with election. He famously said that he could wish all his works would be lost save only the catechism for children and *The Bondage of the Will*. It is those works that focus most clearly on salvation by grace, and grace alone. It is those works that allow for Christian freedom and the enjoyment of God's creation. We are not bureaucrats in the Department of Salvation. We are not cubicle dwellers who must trudge through one sharing of the gospel after another and never giving thought to any other matter. We are the sons of the free woman. We are the free children of God. [Referring to Luther's famous remark that Luther, after having first preached the word, could then] sit in Wittenberg and drink beer while the Spirit does his work through the Word. We can go fishing and play racket ball take a walk with our [spouses] and worry about how the Huskers will do this fall. It is for freedom that Christ has set us free.

And glory of glories—in all this the Lord has chosen to use us for his purposes. And his purposes are many. That he might have more children to love, he sets us in families and blesses us to be fruitful and multiply. That men might serve one another as Christ serves us, he gives us each a vocation and a place of service to others as butchers and bakers and candlestick makers. And that his word might go forth, he calls some to be preachers in his church and provides for them through generosity of the people. In all these things, God delights to bless us by doing his good works through us.

Why preach? Why give? How can we not? We who died to sin, how can we live in it any longer? We who are saved by grace, how can we resist giving a reason for this hope we have within to all who ask? We do not do good works to earn salvation, our own or another's, but because we are the Father's children and we love to please the Father. We do not spread the Gospel to collect feathers in our cap, or out of fear that God might lose one of his elect if we don't, but because we live and breathe and have our being in this Gospel. A father loves his son just because. A preacher preaches just because. A Christian prays just because. If any mercenary thought, any extortion, any "or else" enters into such things they cease to be what they are and we are held again under the Law, coercion, and sin.[10]

Every child of God will experience unmerited bliss in heaven forevermore. As Pieper puts it, "There are no degrees of bliss [in heaven] because all of the blessed are perfectly happy."[11] Christ stands in and completely covers us when we are judged according to works. Exactly how is not entirely explained in Scripture. Because our reward encompasses the fruit we bear in the power of Christ following justification, he and other Reformational theologians indicate that there may be degrees of glory (as opposed to bliss) "for work and fidelity,"[12] particularly in the face of suffering, or, as others have put it, according to capacities and responsibilities. Justin Taylor writes:

> All true believers will receive the great reward of seeing God face to face, and this should motivate all of our actions. The NT nowhere clearly and explicitly teaches varying degrees of reward, though this may indeed be true. If so, some may have greater capacities as well as greater responsibilities, but all of us will experience "fullness of joy" and "pleasures forevermore" at God's right hand (Ps. 16:11). Maranatha—come quickly, Lord Jesus![13]

This leads us to the second error Christians are prone to fall into—ascribing the presence of a negative or punishing aspect to heaven when we allow even the possibility that the reward might vary among people. Our sinful human nature is so warped and we are so turned in on ourselves that we start to choke at even the thought of any type of variation in reward. In our envy we shake our fist at the audacity of God for even possibly dishing out some type of blessing that is not absolutely equal in all respects.

Again, we know the criteria for judgment. It is based upon perfect compliance with the general covenant of works set forth throughout

---

10. Curtis, "Liturgy as Beacon for the Elect," 10–12 (used by permission).
11. Pieper, *Christian Dogmatics*, vol. 3, 552f.
12. Ibid.
13. Stark, quoting Justin Taylor, "You Asked."

Scripture. In the judgment, we are rewarded according to what we have done. The Christian standing before that judgment seat is clothed with the white robe of Christ's imputed gift of righteousness. The judgment seat for the Christian becomes God's mercy seat. Exactly how Christ's righteousness covers us here is somewhat cryptic in Scripture. Insofar as he is crowning the perfect righteous obedient good works of Jesus imputed to all believers—that's easy for us to understand and accept. As he also includes what Christ accomplishes in and through us following justification, as part of his work in sanctifying and glorifying us, that's easy too, if we share the reward equally. Professor Blomberg examines all of the biblical data regarding our reward and makes a compelling biblical case that all believers will realize their reward in a totally equal way in heaven.[14] If, however, it is partly according to what he has tangibly accomplished in and through us, subject to variation among individuals, that becomes more difficult for us to get our heads around in a gracious way without envy setting in. In this regard, we are simply not given the formula based on our current understanding of Scripture.

Jonathan Edwards believed that there will be variation to the extent that people are of differing capacities. He believed that we all will be filled with our brims overflowing like different sized cups being dipped in the vast ocean. No one will be dissatisfied for there all will be filled with untold riches.[15] Many, if not most Reformational theologians seem to be in general agreement here. This view is fairly acceptable even to our flawed sensibilities. If I'm not good at algebra, would I really need or want to be awarded an extensive algebra library like my math professor? In the example above, for the kid who loved mowing the lawn with the father and was a natural at landscaping, wouldn't it be perfectly appropriate if his reward was tailored to that, as he grew to maturity? Perhaps another one of the children loved "driving" the jeep together with their father as they held the steering wheel together. (Don't try any of this at home.) Perhaps her or his reward would be tailored to that and how she or he is constituted as a unique human being. Or, if there are variations due to our level of suffering, would I begrudge a fellow believer a special crown of commendation for having been torched to death as a human candle in Nero's garden? Would I begrudge the martyr Polycarp a larger yacht? Would it be wrong for the apostles to be honored for the office given them and the suffering they endured on account of it?

14. See Blomberg, "Degrees of Reward."
15. See Stark, quoting Justin Taylor, "You Asked."

This is not to definitively and specifically say how it will be. We must continue to thoroughly examine what Scripture says. To go beyond Scripture would be speculative. This is simply to demonstrate that, on the basis of what Scripture has clearly revealed, whether we understand it to be equal in all respects or not, the distribution of gifts would be "part of the party"[16], the great celebration. One thing is clear. It will *all* be good. There will be nothing bad in heaven. It will *all* be really, really good. There will be no such things as a bad seat at the stadium or being assigned living quarters at a grungy rooming house. There will be nothing hellish in heaven. It will be all blessing and no curse. If there is to be variation of blessing, it need not have a negative connotation. Moreover, even assuming for a moment that the judgment will be varied according to the varied good works reflected in our lives, which ones would even be counted? For a good work to be truly good, it must be propelled by a perfect motivation, having not even a scintilla of sinful self-interest. Therefore, no work of ours is ever good except as filtered through the righteousness of Christ. That ought to deeply humble all of us.

God reveals the fact of our heavenly inheritance, including the idea of a heavenly reward to us, for our mutual comfort and encouragement, not to instigate sibling rivalry, one-upmanship or one-downmanship (i.e., if many who are last are going to be first, well then, I'm going to be the most humble person that ever lived!). The issue here seems very close to the "why many and not others" question concerning the issue of salvation/election itself. Of course, there the real question is: "why any?" Similarly here, if there are differing levels of reward according to what God has tangibly accomplished in each of our individual lives following justification, the question ought not to be "why not less for them and more for me?" but rather, "why is any of this estate for them or me?" Moreover, once he completes the work he began in us and we are all glorified, it would appear that everyone may catch up anyway!

Part of the difficulty here lies in the tension between the present age and the age to come. Once we are fully justified before God, our good works arise out of our salvation; they are not done for salvation. In this age, through Jesus Christ, truly good works before God are possible for the first time as we anticipate the age to come. It ought not to trouble us that there is fruit (reward) to selfless obedience. It's what Adam and Eve could originally enjoy and what will become a way of life when we are glorified in sinless perfection. In heaven we will be in a perfect state of blessed

---

16. Horton, "Questions and Answers."

Part 3: Some Additional Liberating Applications and Implications

self-forgetfulness enjoying the reward of the fruit of our labor perfectly. In this age we cannot perform perfectly or even think about these things without tainting the whole enterprise. Until we are glorified, we need the purifying filter of Jesus Christ to cleanse even our best thoughts and works. *Once justified we are in a completely new economy which we already enjoy in this age on account of Christ.*

Besides a total lack of sloth, there will be no envy, jealousy or sibling rivalry in heaven. We will be delivered from this curved-in-on-itself body of death. There will be no dissatisfaction in heaven. The meek shall inherit the whole earth. We will all be blessed beyond measure on account of our Savior. It is difficult to see and comprehend beyond our sinful selfish natures. When wealthy parents die, each child naturally wants to be the favored one that inherits the summer home. Christians need to move beyond this mindset and keep our eyes fixed on Jesus who will provide for each one more than he or she could ever imagine or hope for. The final fullness of our salvation will one day be revealed: "What no eye has seen, what no ear has heard, and what no human mind has conceived—the things God has prepared for those who love him" (1 Cor 2:9 NIV). We have all we need in Christ without trying to get favorite child status from the Father or eternal adulation from our neighbors for whatever accolades we might receive.

Our inheritance is unfathomable. Our heavenly Father is the ultimate multi-trillionaire of the universe and we are promised to inherit the earth (Matt 5; Rev 5). As Todd Wilken once put it: "No one gets gypped! Not a single person gets gypped!"[17] Rejoice in the promised certainty of your heavenly reward and let it propel you. Cheer up and don't let anyone rain on this parade. In Christ, as wild shoots grafted on to the vine, we are all heirs of a truly wild and crazy inheritance. *He unites us to himself, channels his enabling grace through us to walk in good works and then rewards our good works, not based on our efforts, but as part of our inheritance on account of his promise!* Accept it with childlike faith, understanding that none of us have yet matured to full sanctification and glorification. Remember the adopted children and their dad "pushing" the lawnmower and "driving" the jeep and stop taking ourselves so seriously. Though in this present life we are simultaneously saint and sinner, everyone entering into heaven will hear the same words on account of Christ: "Well done, good and faithful servant" (Matt 25: 14–30; Luke 19: 11–27). It's either, "Come, you who are blessed by my Father, inherit the kingdom prepared for you from the

---

17. Wilken, "Listener Email and the Issues, Etc. Comment Line, 5/3/13."

foundation of the world," or, "I never knew you; depart from me" (Matt 25: 30–46; Matt 7:23; Luke 13:27). There is no third category. All of his children will receive the reward of the inheritance (Col 3:24). "Rejoice and be glad for your reward is great in heaven!" (Matt 5:12; 1 Pet 1:3–9).

Conclusion
Lennon and McCartney, John Paul, or John and Paul?

DUE TO THE CURRENT state of Protestant evangelicalism, particularly the anti-institutional, anti-formal, anti-authority effects the hippie culture has had upon it, there are some evangelicals who are now opting for Roman Catholicism (as well as Eastern Orthodoxy). Moreover, much of evangelicalism itself has embraced the Roman Catholic church as a sister church. While this book has focused primarily on the need for reformation in evangelicalism (both pop evangelicalism and the distorted, legalistic, stoic version of Reformational evangelicalism), the need for reformation of the Roman Catholic church (not to mention the Eastern Orthodox church and the Protestant liberal church) continues, as well.

There is still much to protest against in the Roman Catholic church. This includes, among other things: the Papacy, belief in purgatory, indulgences, invoking the saints, Mariology, transubstantiation, monasteries, relics, shrines, forbidding the clergy to marry, and, denying the five *solas* of the Reformation which was memorialized at the Council of Trent. The most significant difference continues to be the doctrine of justification, i.e., how one is made right before a Holy God. The Roman Catholic church still includes human merit as part of the equation, which is what triggered the Reformation in the first place. Though less crass than medieval practices, Rome continues to burden people's consciences by having them perform works to merit the merits of Christ. As long as such unbiblical burdening of consciences continues, there will be, God willing, Reformation churches protesting. Good works are crucial, but they are the fruit of sanctification, not a root of justification. Justification precedes sanctification, not the other

CONCLUSION

way around. Moreover, Christ's meritorious work is *the* root of our justification, sanctification and glorification.

Having said that, this is not to say that a Roman Catholic cannot be considered a brother or sister in Christ. Going all the way back to Luther and Calvin, the Reformers have always recognized a body of true believers within the walls of Roman Catholicism, notwithstanding their condemnation of the conduct of the institution itself. The institution of the Roman Catholic Church, however, does continue in its digression from the clear teachings of Scripture by many of its own pronouncements which it has yet to retract.

Therefore, the way forward for the church is neither with an evangelical church that remains saturated with the John and Paul of Lennon and McCartney, nor with the yet unreformed Roman church of the late Pope John Paul II. There is another John and Paul to whose teachings the church must continue to yield her allegiance—not only John and Paul, but Peter, James, and the other apostles, as well. As John wrote, quoting Jesus, "If you abide in my word, you are truly my disciples, and you will know the truth, and the truth will set you free" (John 8:31–32); and, as Paul wrote, "And to the one who does not work but believes in him who justifies the ungodly, his faith is counted as righteousness" (Rom 4:5). We need to once again fully recover the apostles' teachings that John Calvin and Martin Luther had recovered in the Protestant Reformation. Now, if only Hans and Margarethe Luther had named their son Paul instead of Martin . . . ☺

Bibliography

Acuff, Jon. "Hand Raising Worship—the 10 Styles." *Stuff Christians Like* (blog), posted July 14, 2008. http://stuffchristianslike.net/2008/07/14/345-hand-raising-worship-the-10-styles.

"Begg, Horton, Lawson, Mohler, and Sproul: Questions and Answers #2." 2010 Ligonier National Conference. Youtube video, 1:12:52, posted September 10, 2013. https://www.youtube.com/watch?v=-jcZJ_moMyA.

Blomberg, Craig L. "Degrees of Reward in the Kingdom of Heaven?" *Journal of the Evangelical Theological Society* 35 (1992) 159–72.

Calvin, John. *Commentary on the Book of Psalms*. Text courtesy of Christian Classics Etherial Library. http://biblehub.com/commentaries/calvin/psalms/42.htm.

———. *Institutes of the Christian Religion*. Translated by Henry Beveridge. Vols. 1–2. Grand Rapids: Eerdmans, 1957.

Cole, Amaris. "Billy Graham: A Secret Anglican?" *Anglican Ink*, posted September 11, 2014. http://www.anglican.ink/article/billy-graham-secret-anglican.

Curtis, H. R. "The Liturgy as Beacon for the Elect." Presented at the Gottesdienst West Conference in Ravenna, NE, June 18, 2010. Used by permission. http://www.scribd.com/doc/33702693/Liturgy-as-Beacon-for-God-s-Elect-Gottesdienst-West-2010.

Fisk, Jonathan. "Glawspel Redux." *Worldview Everlasting* (blog) video, 8:22, posted July 9, 2013. http://www.worldvieweverlasting.com/2013/07/09/doublestrike-glawspel-redux.

Fitzpatrick, Elyse. On "Parenting with Discipline and Grace." *White Horse Inn* (podcast) episode 1121, September 30, 2012.

Hicks, Zac. "Is 'God Inhabits the Praises of His People' Really Biblical?" Hicks's blog, posted January 24, 2012. http://www.zachicks.com/blog/2012/1/24/is-god-inhabits-the-praises-of-his-people-really-biblical.html.

Horton, Michael. *A Better Way: Rediscovering the Drama of Christ-Centered Worship*. Grand Rapids: Baker, 2002.

———. *The Christian Faith: A Systematic Theology for Pilgrims on the Way*. Grand Rapids: Zondervan, 2011. Used by permission.

———. *The Gospel Commission: Recovering God's Strategy for Making Disciples*. Grand Rapids: Baker, 2011.

———. *The Gospel-Driven Life*. Grand Rapids: Baker, 2009.

———. "Missional Church or New Monasticism?" *Modern Reformation* 20 (2011) 14–21.

Bibliography

———. On "The Lord's Prayer" (part 1). *White Horse Inn* (podcast) episode 1093, March 18, 2012. https://www.whitehorseinn.org/blog/entry/2012-show-archive/2012/03/18/whi-1093-the-lords-prayer-part-1.

———. *People and Place: A Covenant Ecclesiology*. Louisville: Westminster John Knox, 2008.

———. "Your Own Personal Jesus." *Modern Reformation* 17 (2008) 14–20.

Jones, Ken. On "Rightly Dividing the Word: Law & Gospel." *White Horse Inn* (podcast) episode 946, May 24, 2009.

Jones, Peter. *The Other Worldview: Exposing Christianity's Greatest Threat*. Bellingham, WA: Kirkdale, 2015.

Keller, Timothy. *The Prodigal God: Recovering the Heart of the Christian Faith*. New York: Dutton, 2008.

Lee, Brian J. "Why We Seek to Know God's Will." *Modern Reformation* 13 (2004) 33.

Lewis, C. S. *Weight of Glory and Other Addresses*. New York: Touchstone, 1996.

Maas, Korey. "On Being Well-Dressed: A New Year's Dialogue." *Modern Reformation* 12 (2003) 17–19, 25.

Metaxas, Eric. "How Sweet Will Be the Flower: The Life and Death of NBC's David Bloom." Originally published 2003. http://ericmetaxas.com/writing/essays/david-bloom-1963-2003.

Nesch, Elliot. "Church of Tares: Purpose Driven, Seeker Sensitive, Church Growth & New World Order." Youtube video, 1:59:26, posted November 20, 2012. https://www.youtube.com/watch?v=kxY3VbBHTkY.

Packer, J. I. "Rooted and Built Up in Christ (Col. 2:6–7): The Prayer Book Path." Address given at St. Paul's Church, Bloor Street, Toronto, May 1, 1999. http://prayerbook.ca/resources/onlinelibrary/prayer-book-yesterday-today-tomorrow/#rootedandbuiltupinchrist.

Palmer, Edwin H. *The Holy Spirit: His Person and Ministry*. Phillipsburg, NJ: Presbyterian & Reformed, 1974.

Pieper, Francis. *Christian Dogmatics*. Vol. 3. St. Louis: Concordia, 2011.

Psalter Hymnal: Doctrinal Standards and Liturgy of the Christian Reformed Church. Grand Rapids: Board of Publications of the CRC, 1976.

Reformed Churchmen. "Crown Him with Many Crowns: Westminster Abbey (Hillbillies Disallowed)." Video, 3:35, posted September 29, 2012. http://reformationanglicanism.blogspot.com/2012/09/crown-him-with-many-crowns-westminster.html.

Rhode, Jeremy. "The Gospel for Former [Pop] Evangelicals: The Divine Service." *Issues, Etc.* (podcast), October 26, 2011. http://issuesetc.org/2011/10/26/the-gospel-for-former-evangelicals-the-divine-service-with-pr-jeremy-rhode-10262011.

Riddlebarger, Kim. *A Case for Amillennialism*. Grand Rapids: Baker and Intervarsity, 2003.

———. On "Worldliness." *White Horse Inn* (podcast), originally aired July 3, 2005.

Rosenbladt, Rod. On "Creed or Chaos?" *White Horse Inn* (podcast) episode 915, October 19, 2008.

Rosebrough, Chris. "Resistance Is Futile: You Will Be Assimilated into the Community." *Fighting for the Faith* (radio podcast), May 11, 2012. http://crosebrough.typepad.com/fightingforthefaith/2012/05/resistance-is-futile-you-will-be-assimilated-into-the-community.html.

Smith, James K. A. "An Open Letter to Praise Bands." *Fors Clavigera* (blog), posted February 20, 2012. http://forsclavigera.blogspot.com/2012/02/open-letter-to-praise-bands.html.

Bibliography

Sproul, R. C. *The Holiness of God*. Wheaton, IL: Tyndale, 1985.

Tchividjian, Tullian. "The Good News of Final Judgement." August 12, 2013. Quoting Jonathan Linebaugh. http://liberatenet.org/2013/08/12the-good-news-of-final-judgement-2. Source no longer available.

———. *Jesus + Nothing = Everything*. Wheaton, IL: Crossway, 2011.

———. *One Way Love: Inexhaustible Grace for an Exhausted World*. Colorado Springs: Cook, 2013.

Triglot Concordia: The Symbolical Books of the Evangelical Lutheran Church. Text in German, Latin, and English. St. Louis: Concordia, 1921. http://bookofconcord.org.

Trinity Hymnal. Orthodox Presbyterian Church. Suwanee, GA: Great Commission, 1990.

Wells, David. On "The Courage to Be Protestant." *White Horse Inn* (podcast) episode 913, October 5, 2008.

Wilken, Todd. "Behind the Music: The Real Worship War." *Issues, Etc.* (journal), fall 2012. http://issuesetc.org/wp-content/uploads/2012/09/FALL-2012.pdf.

———. "Listener Email and the Issues, Etc. Comment Line, 11/1/12." *Issues, Etc.* (podcast). http://issuesetc.org/2012/11/01/1-listener-email-and-the-issues-etc-comment-line-11112.

———. "Listener Email and the Issues, Etc. Comment Line, 5/3/13." *Issues, Etc.* (podcast). http://issuesetc.org/2013/05/03/2-listener-email-and-the-issues-etc-comment-line-5313.

Williamson, G. I. *The Westminster Confession of Faith for Study Classes*. Phillipsburg, NJ: Presbyterian & Reformed, 1964.

Zahl, Paul F. M. *New Persuasive Words for Defaced or Degraded Ones: Mercy, Grace and Hope in an Age of Recession*. DVD. Mockingbird Ministries, 2010.

www.ingramcontent.com/pod-product-compliance
Lightning Source LLC
Chambersburg PA
CBHW072137160426
43197CB00012B/2148